INFORMATION ACCESS, TOOLS, SERVICES AND SYSTEMS

INFORMATION ACCESS, TOOLS, SERVICES AND SYSTEMS

G. Devarajan
and
Joseph Kurien Pulikuthiel

Ess Ess Publications
New Delhi

Information Access, Tools, Services and Systems

ISBN : 978-81-7000-628-2

Rs.650/-

First Published 2011

Published by:
Ess Ess Publications
4837/24, Ansari Road,
Darya Ganj,
New Delhi-110 002.
INDIA
Phones: 23260807, 41563444
Fax: 41563334
E-mail: info@essessreference.com
www.essessreference.com

Cover Design by *Patch Creative Unit*

Printed and bound in India at Salasar Imaging Systems.

Dedicated
In Memory
of
Prof.K.A.Isaac
Doyen of Library Science Education in India

Contents

Preface

"Knowledge is power", said Socrates, the greatest of the Greek pedagogues and philosophers. By raising the questions like "why, how, and what", he delved deep into the fundamental questions concerned with epistemology and logic. In the modern era of a deluge of data and isolated pieces of information, how can one who seeks information, derive the right knowledge at the right time? All economic, political, social and moral endeavours of man can succeed only if you possess the right kind of information. This humble attempt by us depicts the different paths to arrive at the right information for all type of readers, scientists, researchers, teachers, librarians and information scientists. The various aspects of conventional information sources like books, journals, serials, conference proceedings and the modern databases are discussed and presented to everyone concerned with the use of information. A detailed treatise on information sources, services access tools, reference service, user studies, user education, bibliographic control, information services and information systems and products are presented in the context of modern developments in information, communication and computer technology. This book has been specially intended for the library and information students and teachers, working librarians and information scientists and the scientific community in general. We would be immensely gratified if this work enhances the cause which they strive for.

The authors record their appreciation and profound thanks to Mr.Sumit Sethi, M/S Ess Ess Publications, New Delhi for bringing out this book in good format within record time.

Prof (Dr). G. Devarajan
Joseph Kurien Pulikuthiel

Trivandrum
01 .8.2010

Chapter 1

Information

Information is a vital resource in today's society which hardly needs emphasis as it brings people and thought together. It is considered as the fourth resource, the other three being people, money and physical resources. It is also considered as fifth basic human needs in the order, air, water, food and shelter. It is an indispensable raw material for right decision-making from governmental level to the personal level. It is a well accepted generalization that a country which is rich in information is rich in the socio-economic spheres. Information is dividing the world between fast moving economies that make effective use of information and slow moving economies that do not use it. The backwardness of any country in respect of socio-economic spheres is mainly due to lack of adequate information especially in the field of Science and technology. The significance of information paved the way for development of Science information and technologies to manage information. In fact information has a synergizing effect in a number of human activities in the educational, scientific, technological and societal spheres. Thus one can realize that information is an all pervasive resource and helps in establishing a continuum from the past to present and finally to the future. In this chapter an attempt is made to discuss the concepts Information, Information Science, Information technology and Informatics in their various ramifications.

INFORMATION

The word 'information' is derived from Latin word, 'Informare' means giving shape to something. There are a number of terms such as knowledge, facts, data, news, message etc used in common parlance as synonyms or near synonyms to 'information'. But none of these terms are equivalent to information. In fact it is very difficult to define information precisely. According to the Oxford English Dictionary: i)Information is the action of informing; formation or moulding the mind or character, training, instruction, teaching; communication of instructive knowledge; ii) the action of informing; communication of the knowledge of "news" of some fact or occurrence; the action of telling or fact of being told of something; and iii) knowledge communicated concerning some particular fact, subject or event; that of which one is apprised or told; intelligence, news. Van Nostrand's Scientific Encyclopedia gives the concept of information as "a collection of facts or other data especially as derived from the processing of data "Whereas, it is an assemblage of data in a comprehensible form recorded on paper or some other medium, and capable of communication. A number of authors have attempted to define information. According to Shera, information, both in the sense it is used by the biologists and in the sense librarians use it, is a "fact". It is the stimuli we receive through our senses. It may be an isolated fact or a whole cluster of facts; but it is still a unit; it is a unit of thought. In the words of prof. Bhattacharyya, information is the message conveyed or intended to be conveyed by a systematised body of ideas, or its accepted or acceptable substitutes. Information is the meaning that a human expresses by, or extracts from, representation of facts and ideas by means of the known conventions of the representation used. According to Faibisoff and Dely "information is an idea. It is a symbol or a set of symbols which have the potential for meaning".

Information can be defined as "some meaningful message recorded in conventional or non conventional media and stored and processed by messages and their dissemination to users". Mc Pherson states that information permeates all organizations, it is the raw metatarsal of cognitive activity.... the means whereby organization obtains its window on the world. In fact it is a diffused resource. Horton defines information in the context of treating it as a resource:

- Something of fundamental value, like money, capital goods, labour or raw materials;
- Something with specifiable and measurable characteristics, such as method of collection, utilities and uses, a life cycle pattern with different attributes at each stage, and interchangeability with other resources;
- An input, which can be transferred into useful outputs;
- Something that presents to top management a variety of development choices.

McGarry has tried to provide the varied attributes of 'information' rather than defining information. He provides the following attributes to information. i) Information can be regarded as a near synonym of fact. ii) It has a transforming or reinforcing effect on what is known or believed to be known by a human being; iii) Information is used as an aid in decision making; iv) Information is the freedom of choice one has in selecting message; v) Information is a necessary piece of "something" when we are faced with a choice. The amount required depends upon the complexity of the decision to be made; vi) Information is the raw material from which knowledge is derived; vii) Information is exchanged with outer world; not merely received; and viii) Information can be defined in terms of its effect on the receipient. It is seen that a comprehensive definition of the concept 'information' is not possible due to its amorphous, slippery, complex and multifarious nature. To quote T. N. Rajan, no universally accepted definition of information is yet crystallised perhaps it will never be crystallized.

INFORMATION, KNOWLEDGE AND WISDOM

The relationship between knowledge and information is given in the Random House Dictionary of English Language as "knowledge communicated or received concerning a particular fact or circumstance; any knowledge gained through communication, research, instruction is information. Information and knowledge are distinguished as follows:

i) information is piecemeal, fragmented, particular, whereas knowledge is structural, coherent and universal;

ii) Information is timely, transitory, perhaps even ephemeral, whereas knowledge is of enduring significance.

iii) Information is a flow of messages, whereas knowledge is a stock largely resulting from the flow in the sense that the input of information may affect the stock of knowledge by adding to it, restructuring it or changing it in anyway (though conceivably information may leave knowledge unchanged).

In the words of Brookes knowledge is a summation of many bits of "information" which are organised into some sort of coherent entity. The relationship is represented by means of a simple equation, which Brookes calls the "fundamental equation of information Science".

$$K(s) + AI = K(S + AS)$$

Here K(s) is knowledge sturcture and K(S + AS) is the modified knowledge sturcture caused by absorption of the increment of information of K(S). Brookes believes that correct solution of this equation and its proper interpretation may enable us to fully explain information process.

T. S Eliot brought the relationship between information, knowledge and wisdom in poetical lines as: Where is the wisdom ? We have lost in knowledge. Where is the knowledge? We have lost in data. Knowledge has more profound connotation when compared with information. Knowledge can carry with it the idea that apparently objective information is filtered and conditioned in transmission, by individual life-experiences and social values. Society forms the alchemic process by which base "information" is transmuted into "knowledge". Thus a conceptual framework built up from the idea of "knowledge" will include a socio-cultural dimension which might be omitted from a framework built up from the more reductive idea of "information". However, it is accepted that, given the current popularity of the word and the fact that it is commonly used interchangeably with the word "knowledge", information is the word that is more likely to be used. Knowledge is like light weightless and intangible, it can easily travel the world, enlightening the lives of people everywhere.

TYPES OF INFORMATION

There are various types or forms of information. These types are recognized on the basis of different characteristic features. According to Prof, Bhattacharyya information has two recognizable varieties viz i) Discursive; and ii) Non-Discursive information. Discursive information is the message conveyed by a systematised body of ideas or its accepted or acceptable substitutes. The information that is not discursive is non-discursive information. Non-discursive information is of two types: Qualitative and quantitative information. Information can be categorised on the basis of the nature of its use and purpose for which it is used. J. H. Shera has categorised information into six types. They are: i) Conceptual information ii) empirical information iii) procedural information iv) stimulatory information v) policy information; and vi) directive information.

The Social Scientists categorise information as: i) statistical information; ii) descriptive information iii) analytical information. The population data of a country can be considered example of statistical information. If someone describes the growth of population that has taken place in various periods that will constitute descriptive information whereas if someone analyses and interprets the above statistical information that will result into analytical information or interpretative information.

Saracevic and Wood have categorized information based on developmental needs as : i)Scientific and technical information; ii) policy and management information; and iii) operational and industrial information. Information is categorized based on its use in various human activities such as: i)Technical information; ii)Environmental information; iii) Economic information; iv)Geographical information ; v) Climatological information ;and vi)Socio-cultural information.

QUALITIES OF INFORMATION

Information has varied attributes and qualities. Cleveland in an address to the World future Society in 1982, outlined the inherent characteristics of information. He applied the following seven objectives to qualify information: human, expandable, compressible, substitutable, transportable, diffusive and shareable. As a vital resource, information ought to have certain ideal qualities also. They are:

i) Accessibility;

ii) Comprehensiveness;

iii) Precision;

iv) Compatibility;

v) Timeliness;

vi) Clarity;

vii) Flexibility;

viii) Verifiability;

ix) Free of bias; and

x) Quantifiable.

William F William has recognised six parameters of information. They are: a)Quantity of information which can be measured by the number of documents, pages, words, characters, bits, drawings etc; b)Content, the meaning of information; c)Structure, the organisation of information and its logical relationship between statements or elements; d)Language, symbols, alphabets, codes and syntax with which the ideas are expressed; e)Quality, that which characterizes the completeness, accuracy, relevance and timeliness of information; and f)Life, the total span of time in which value can be derived from the information.

PRINCIPLES OF INFORMATION

The basic principles of librarianship are focused in the Five laws of Library Science enunciated by Dr. S. R. Ranganathan, the luminary in the field. On the analogy of Five laws of Library Science, Prof. Bhattacharyya formulated Five principles of Information viz i)Information is for use; ii)Every information user his/her information; iii)Every piece of information its user; iv)Save the time of the information user; and v)The universe of information is ever growing. These principles underline that information should be put into active use and it should be channelised to the right user at the right time in the right form. This will ultimately result in the growth of universe of nascent information and will be helpful for all pervasive growth in all spheres of human activities.

AGENCIES OF INFORMATION GENERATION

Information is an outcome of various intellectual activities of human beings. The information generation activities are made by individuals, organisations, learned bodies and Governmental agencies. Research and developmental activities carried out by individual research and team research in R & D organisations generate quite a lot of nascent information in the fields of Science and technology, Humanities and Social Sciences. The establishment of various types of R & D institutions immediately after the Second world war all over the world geared up research activities on various subjects. In addition to research institutions a number of academic institutions like universities and colleges entered the arena of academic research which also produced a lot of information. Government is another agency which generates enormous information. Local Governments, State Governments, Central Government, Government departments etc are agencies involved in the generation of new information. These are generated as Census reports, administration reports, rules and regulations, Bills and Acts etc.

In addition to the above said agencies for generation of information, business and industrial organisations generate a lot of information in the field of various commercial sectors and industrial fields. The information generated by such agencies is used for commercial and industrial development.

MEDIA OF INFORMATION

Information is generated through a number of communication channels or media. It is transmitted through printed media viz books and periodicals and mass media viz news papers, radio, Television, cinema etc. These media disseminate a large quantity of information. In the case of printed media 20th century witnessed an exponential growth. It is calculated that the number of articles published in journals each year in the field of Science and Technology alone exceeds one million. It is estimated that literature doubles within a range of 5-10 years in Science and Technology and in a range of 7-13 years in Social Science subjects. In subjects like Computer Science the rate of doubling literature is faster i. e. 1-2 years. It is interesting to note that the growth of literature at the global level is roughly three times faster than the growth of population. In the case of mass media also growth rate is high because of extensive use of these media. It may be said that today we are living in an age of "information explosion" or "information boom" due to information overload or information flood. The major factors leading to this phenomenon are exponential growth of literature, technological developments in printing technology, revolution in the field of information technology.

The information explosion and information flood have created quite a number of problems to information managers in the management of information exhaustively, expeditiously, pin-pointedly and precisely. Of course, information explosion is an opportunity to developed countries and a threat for Third world countries. Together with information explosion we are also confronted with another problem, "information pollution". The proliferation of literature which does not contribute substantially to add knowledge, publication with erroneous information, rehash, cheap publications which exploit the weakness of the society etc. create such a problem. In fact the information users of today are in a state of "information anxiety" and in the state of drowning in information but starving for knowledge.

VALUE OR USES OF INFORMATION

Information is a valuable commodity. The value of information is determined on the basis of providing it to the right user at the right time in the right form with precision. Information is a valuable input to various types of user groups such as students, teachers, researchers, professionals, decision makers, planers etc to satisfy various types of information needs. It is an asset and like other assets and it is useless if it is not put to use. So the value of information is also determined on the basis of how it is utilized. In an information society the importance of information is paramount.

Atherton remarks on the value of information that researchers and scientists necessitates effective communication :

i) To stimulate thought and action by injection of and interaction with, other people's ideas, knowledge, experience and achievements ;

ii) To promote continuous awareness of developments;

iii) To diminish the probability of unwitting duplication of work;

iv) To provide introductory and background information for work at hand ; and

v) To meet specific requirements.

Saracevic and Wood identified the following uses or values of information. It is used for

* Decision making/planning
* Problem solving
* Knowledge competence
* Adaptation
* Productivity
* Efficient and effective use of resources
* Success
* Business
* Research and Development
* Education; and
* Self fulfillment and advancement of individuals.

INFORMATION SOCIETY

The society which depends on information for all its developments is popularly known as information society. Information societies have three main characteristics. They are i) Information is used as an economic resource. Organisations make greater use of information to increase their efficiency, to stimulate innovation and to increase their efficiency, and to increase their effectiveness and competitive position, often through improvements in the quality of the goods and services that they produce. There is also a trend towards the development of more information-intensive organisations that add greater amounts of value and thus benefit a country's overall economy; ii) it is possible to identify greater use of information among the general public. People use information more intensively in their activities as consumers to make their choices between different products, to explore their entitlements to public services, and to take greater control over their own lives. They also use information as citizens to exercise their civil rights and responsibilities; and iii) the development of an information sector within the economy. The function of the information sector is to satisfy the general demand for information facilities and services. A significant part of the sector is concerned with the technological infrastructure the networks of telecommunications and computers.

INFORMATION AGE

Information age refers to modern times, in which getting and giving the right information is the driving force of the society. The rapid growth of the technology we use to access information has moved the world away from that of mechanization and industrialization and towards a truly global economy based on the flow of information. The information age also commonly known as the computer age or computer era is an idea that the current age will be characterized by the ability of individuals to transfer information freely and to have instant access to knowledge that would have been difficult or impossible to find previously. The idea is linked to the concept of digital age or digital revolution and carries the ramifications of a shift from traditional industry that the industrial revolution brought through industrialization to an economy based on the manipulation of information.

INFORMETRICS

According to Brookes, the term Informetrics was first proposed by Otto Nacke of West Germany in 1979. An FID Committee with very broadly defined objectives in the provision of research and technical data gave this name. However, the term was not widely adopted until 1987 when B. C. Brookes at the First Conference on Bibliometrics and Theoretical Aspects of Information Retrieval held at Belgium, suggested that the term "Informetrics" be included in the name of the Second International conference on the subject. Tague-Sutcliffe defines informetrics as "the study of the quantitative aspects of information in any form, not just records or bibliographies, and in any social group, not just scientists. It can incorporate, utilize and extend the many studies of the measurement of information that lies outside the boundaries of both Bibliometrics and Scientometrics, and she continues to say that, although in practice the scope of informetrics is very broad.

INFORMATION THEORY

Information theory is the mathematical study of the transmission, reception, storage and retrieval of information based on the statistical analysis of communication between humans and machines. It is a branch of applied mathematics and electrical engineering involving the quantification of information. Information theory was developed by Claude E Shannon to find fundamental limits on signal processing operations such as compressing data and on reliably storing and communicating data. Since its inception it has broadened to find applications in many other areas including statistical inference, natural language processing, cryptography generally, networks other than communication networks - as in neurobiology, the evolution and function of molecular codes, model selection in ecology, thermal physics, quantum computing, plagiarism detection and other forms of data analysis.

INFORMATION AUDIT

Information Audit is a popular concept in library science literature. It is the examination and evaluation of existing information sources, services and products in an organisation, with a view to developing a strategy for their more efficient and effective preparation, promotion, use or marketing.

In its most precise sense an information audit is that process by which a physical verification and examination of the total information assets within an organization takes place, to ensure that information resources which have been acquired by an organization can be accounted for and located. It is now common practice to define the information audit much more widely, to include the initial examination of resources as described above. This results in an inventory of information resources, then building on that to explore the way in which information flows and knowledge is shared throughout an organization: the mechanisms and channels used, the information needs of the organization's members and the staffing requirement in terms of knowledge and skills to ensure that the organization's total intellectual capital is managed and exploited to maximum efficiency.

The idea of information audit is derived from financial audit in accounting, which as Ellis et al noted, are generally 'compliance' audits, undertaken to ensure that the organization is adhering to proper fiscal and legal standards in its financial management. Information audit takes more the character of 'advisory' audits, which are, more concerned with informing users of existing systems and practices and with assessing the appropriateness of existing systems, standards and practices to the organization's goal or objectives.

Becker (1990) describes five types of information audit:

i) Those based on cost-benefit model;

ii) Those that seek to map the relationship between resources;

iii) Hybrid approaches (which combine the feature of the first two)

iv) Audits management information; and

v) Operational advisory audits

It is the examination and evaluation of existing information sources, services and products in an organization, with a view to developing a strategy for their more efficient and effective preparation promotion, use or marketing.

The use of processes such as information audits is increasingly recommended as part of the information management task. The term audit is used to indicate that the process is similar to financial audits; finding out what information exist, their value, and who is responsible for managing and exploiting them.

The information audit should be seen as a mapping process which brings together information about who the users are, what information they have access to (both from the library and from the other sources), what their information needs are and how the provision of information services can support those needs. Peter Gillman has outlined the use of information audits to identify abut user needs, and he goes into some detail the rather thorny task of separating user needs and user wants.

Aim and Purpose

The information audit in its broadest sense is seen as a valuable management tool and part of continuous management review to assist in the process of achieving maximum effectiveness of information provision and use. Its intension is to establish the total information resources and knowledge base to which an organization and all its constituent parts have access, of which they can make use and from which they can benefit. The information audit also offers a framework from which to develop a knowledge audit. It aims to consider not only what information is available, but also the means by which information and knowledge are gathered and disseminated throughout the organization, the systems and procedures required for this and the way in which such activities are managed and coordinated. The information audit can form the base from which an organizational information policy can develop. It also provides the platform for long term library and information services, strategic planning and service and development.

Preparation and Planning

What will be needed in advance of the audit itself will be a clear profile of the organization, its current and planned activities and objectives, towards which any future information and knowledge management policy and operation can be directed. Each organization will be different in terms of sector, activities, objectives, structure and management style. Therefore the profile will assist in the choice of audit methods and techniques to be used, the design and content of questionnaires and checklists, and the desired mix of the user sample. Those conducting the audit must identify precisely what it is necessary to investigate, drawing up appropriate checklists of items to be audited. Checklists should also cover related equipments and systems in use, their quantities and location. Questionnaires or interview schedules will have to be prepared at this stage as the basis for subsequent user and usage surveys, and consideration is given to appropriate methods of communication to be used. Decisions will also be required on the amount and type of operational statistics required in support of the final analysis and recommendations.

The Process

Following the initial planning, the first step in the information audit is to carry out a thorough investigation of the information sources and related means of access and retrieval that exist through the organization. If this involves arranging visits to other departments and offices and discussion with individuals, then it is appropriate to combine the first step with the next part of the process of users' information needs analysis.

Gathering this information requires some form of user surveys, usually either by face-to-face interview or by the circulation of a questionnaire. Both methods should take as little of the user's time as possible. This is likely to generate a greater response, as adequate preparation and understanding by all those involved. The Library and Information services website offers a useful means of publicizing the audit and confirming the schedule. In order to ensure maximum co-operation from individuals and departments, appropriate communication of its objectives need to be made beforehand. The purpose and style of the investigation should be put forward in positive terms, emphasizing the ultimate benefits and the value of the user's participation, allowing adequate time for individuals to prepare their response. When the audit has been completed there should be feed back to those who have participated as well as wider dissemination of the results to inform senior management, whose commitment will be essential to future development.

Use and Benefits

Information audits also involve reviews of systems and procedures, analysis of operations, costing and budgeting reviews, and Library and Information Service staff training and development assessment. When an organization is pursuing a quality management policy, the quality manuals and related procedures can act as a valuable source of reference, often suggesting new approaches and solutions to what might have been viewed as long standing problems.

As a management technique the information audit has a lot to offer, particularly if it is used on a regular basis, rather than as a one-off activity. It can act as a monitoring mechanism, providing regular feed back on the quality of both the information itself and its provisions; it will assist in short and long term financial and management planning; it can help to shape overall organizational policy. To achieve this will involve setting up follow-up procedures and activities to ensure: continued two-way communication with users; wider information sharing; ongoing staff development in terms of renewing skills and keeping up to date subject knowledge and sources, as well as professional practice; and continuous awareness of and involvement in the activities of the organization as a whole.

INFORMATION SCIENCE

There are a number of definitions available to explain the discipline, Science of information or information science. According to the Encyclopedia Britanica, Information Science is the discipline that deals with the processes of storing and transferring of information. It attempts to bring together concepts and methods from various disciplines such as library science, computer science, lingustics, cybernetics, and other technologies inorder to develop techniques and devices to aid in the handling -that is, in the storage, control and retrieval of information.

According to Pauline Atherton Information Science is recognised as a complex multidisciplinary subject ranging from computer and telecommunications through cybernetics to psychology, logic and techniques of classification and indexing, and as such the information work and information science may be defined briefly as professional disciplines concerned with the accumulation, storage and transfer of recorded knowledge.

Harrod's Librarians' Glossary defines Information Science as the study of the use of information, its sources and development; usually taken to refer to the role of scientific, industrial, and specialised libraries and information units in the handling and dissemination of information.

Glynn Harmon opines that Information Science evolved not only an expansion or a metamorphosis of documentation and information retrieval, but, also directly or indirectly incorporated or paralled "several prevailing objectives or concepts of the communication and behavioural sciences and other contributory disciplines.

Shera is of the view that librarianship is a generic term and information science is an area of research which draws its substance, methods and techniques from a variety of disciplines to achieve and understanding of the properties, behaviour and flow of information.... Information science contributes to the theoretical and intellectual base for the library operations.

According to Harold Borko, "Information Science is that discipline that investigates the properties and behaviour of information, the forces governing the flow and use of information, and the means of processing information for optimum accessibility and usability. It is concerned with that body of knowledge relating to the origination, collection, organisation, storage, retrieval interpretation, transmission, transformation and utilisation of information. This includes the investigation of information representations in both natural and artificial systems, the use of codes for efficient message, transmission, and the study of information processing devices and techniques such as computers and their programming systems. It is an interdisciplinary science which is derived from and related to such fields as mathematics, logic, lingustics, psychology, computer technology, operations research, the graphic arts, communications, library science, management and other similar fields. It has both a pure science component, which inquires into the subject without regard to its application, and an applied science component, which develops services and products".

INFORMATICS

In Russia and other east European countries, Informatics is used more or less as an equivalent concept to Information Science. It is being used since 1966. The term, informatics is inextricably linked with documents and the information contained in them. According to Harrod's Librarians' Glossary Informatics is: i)the processes, methods and laws relating to the recording, analytical - synthetical processing, storage, retrieval and dissemination of scholarly communication as such which is the attribute of the respective science or discipline; ii)the study of the structure of knowledge and of its embodiment in information handling systems; and iii)the study of the handling and communication of information, particularly by automated and electronic methods.

Informatics is the science of information. It studies the

representation, processing and communication of information in natural and artificial systems. Since computers, individuals and organizations all process information, informatics has computational, cognitive and social aspects.

Informatics is the discipline of science, which investigates the structure and properties (not specific content) of scientific information activity, its theory, history, methodology and organization.

The French term informatique, together with various translations informatics (English), informatik (German) and informatica (Italian, Spanish) was coined by Dreyfus, in March 1962, and refers to the application of computer to store and process information. The morphology, information + -ics uses 'the accepted form for names of sciences as conics, linguistics, tactics'. (Oxford English Dictionary 1989); information encompasses both science and practice. Phonologically, informatics combines elements from both 'information' and 'automatic', which strengthens its semantic appeal.

Scope of Informatics

What are the areas common in informatics: the focus on information and how it is represented, processed and communicated between a variety of systems. Representations include paper, analogue and digital records of texts, sounds and images, as well as, for instance, the information represented in a gene and the memories of an individual or an organization.

Informatics studies the interaction of information with individuals and organizations, as well as the fundamental of computation and computability, and the hardware and software technologies used to store, process and communicate digitized information. It includes the study of communication as a process that links people together, to affect the behaviour of individuals and organizations.

Informatics as a Science

Science progresses by defining, developing, criticizing and refining new concepts, in order to account for observed phenomena. Informatics is developing its own fundamental concepts of communication, knowledge, data, secrecy, interaction and information, relating them to such phenomena as computation, thought and language and applying them to develop tools for the management of information resources.

Informatics has many aspects. It encompasses, and builds on a number of existing academic disciplines: Primarily, Artificial Intelligence, Cognitive Science and Computer Science. Each takes part of informatics as its natural domain. In broad terms, Cognitive Science concerns the study of natural information processing systems, Computer Science concerns the analysis of computation and design of computing systems; and Artificial Intelligence plays a connecting role, producing systems designed to emulate by, other disciplines, such as Mathematics, Electronics, Biology, Linguistics, Psychology and Sociology. Thus informatics provides a link between disciplines with their own methodologies and perspective, bringing together a common scientific paradigm, common engineering methods and a pervasive stimulus from both technological development and practical application.

Informatics builds on a long tradition of work in logic, which provides an analysis of meaning, proof and truth. It draws on probability and statistics to relate data and information, and on the more recent tradition of computer science for abstract models of computation and fundamental notions of computability and complexity.

The science of information provides a new paradigm of scientific analysis, which concentrates on the processing and communication & information rather than focusing on the electrical, optical, mechanical or chemical interactions that embody this activity. Informatics provides accounts of the representation, processing and communication of information, the conceptual basis for applying computing and information technologies to develop new tools for the management of information in diverse areas, and also the basis for beginning to unravel the working of the mind.

INFORMATION TECHNOLOGY

The two words, information and technology, used together, have acquired special meaning and interpretation during 1990s. It is only recently that the term has been used as a collective term for the whole spectrum of technologies providing the ways and means to acquire, store, transmit, retrieve and process information.

According to the Webster's New Encyclopedia, Information technology is the collective term for the various technologies involved in the processing and transmission of information. They include computing, telecommunication and microelectronics. Information technology is a development of information sources handled by computers and communicated by electronic channels, databases can thus be accessed by telephone and television links, and computer output can be transmitted in an electronic format directly to a remote receiver.

Rowley opines that Information technology means the collection, storage, processing, dissemination and use of information. It is not confined to hardware and software, but acknowledges the importance of man and goals he sets for this technology, the values employed in making the choices, the assessment criterion used to decide whether he is controlling and being enriched by it.

UNESCO defines information technology as scientific, technological and engineering disciplines and the management techniques used in information handling and processing; their applications; computers and their interaction with men and machines; and associated social, economic and cultural matters.

Information technology plays a major role in the management of information. By the application of it the modern technological developments are being exploited to record, process, store, transfer and retrieve information. An analysis of the aforesaid definitions will reveal that information technology is a combination of technologies such as computer technology, telecommunication systems and services, micrographic and reprographic technology; and information storage technology.

REFERENCES

Bhattacharyya, G: Information Science : A unified view through a system approach. Calcutta, IASLIC, 1978. p. 18.

Bhattacharyya, G: ibid. p. 19

Borko, H: Information Science: What is it? American Documentation. January, 1968. p. 1.

Bose, H: Information Science: Principles and practice. New Delhi, Sterling, 1986. p. 9.

Devarajan, G, Ed: Bibliometric studies. New Delhi, ESS ESS, 1997. p. 15-16.

Encyclopedia Britanica. ed. 15. v. 6-Micropedia. Chicago, Encyclopedia Britanica Inc. 1993. p. 312.

Harrod's Librarians' Glossary and Reference Book. ed. 5. USA, Gower pub. Co. 1984. p. 376.

Harrod's Librarians' Glossary of terms used in librarianship documentation, and the book crafts and reference Book. Ed. 5. USA, Gower Pub. Co. 1984. p. 378.

Harrod's Librarians' Glossary. ed8. England, Gower, 1995. p. 319.

Ibid. P. 11.

Kumar, PSG: Fundamentals of Information Science. New Delhi. S. Chand and Co. , 1998. p. 13.

Kumar, PSG: ibid. p. 24.

Machlup, F and Mansfield, U: Study of information, interdisciplinary messages. New York, Wiley. 1983. p. 743.

McGarry, KJ: Changing context of information: An introductory analysis. London, Clive Bingly. 1981. p. 13.

Mckee, Bob: Informationstudies. Libr. Ass. Rec. 1986. 88(5)pp. 236-39.

Molhot, Pat: The nature of information and its influence on libraries. Special Libraries. July 1984. p. 247.

Prasher, RG: Information and communication. ILA Bulletin 23(3)1987. p. 18.

Random House Dictionary of English Language. New York, Random House, 1966

Rojas, B A: Information systems for the Scientific Management of Agfricultural Research - Conference on selected issues of Agricultural Research in Latin America. Madrid, 1982. ISNAR. March, 19814.

Rowley, Jennifer E: The basics of information technology. London, Clive Bingly, 1988. p. 1.

Sathyanarayana, R: Information Technology and its facets. New Delhi, Manak, 1996. p. 8.

Shera, JH: The foundation of education for librarianship. New York, Becker & Hayes, 1972.

The Oxford English Dictionary. Ed2. v. 8. Oxford, Clarenden Press, 1989. p. 944.

The World Bank: World Development report: Knowledge for Development, 1998-99 New York, OUP Press. p. 1.

UNESCO: World information report, 1997-98. Paris, UNESCO. pp. 271-72.

Van Nostrand's Scientific Encyclopeadia. Ed. 8. New York, Van Nostrand's and Reinhold. 1994. p. 1701.

Webster's New Encyclopedia. New York, Printice Hall, 1992. p. 565.

William, William F: Principles of automated information retrieval. Illinois, Business press, 1965.

Zorkoczy, P and Heap, N: Information Technology. ed. 4. London, Pitman. 1995. p. 7.

Chapter

2

Sources of Information

The beginning of information sources may be traced to man's earliest attempts to record thoughts, concepts, ideas and events. Popper in his book 'Objective knowledge' recognised a world of objective knowledge which is the totality of all human thought embodied in human artefacts, as in documents and also in music, the arts, the technologies. He recognised the objective knowledge is the world three while the first world is the physical world and the second world is subjective knowledge or mental states. It is believed that the visual records had originated when man first sketched the outline of animal that he wished to hunt. Such visual records helped him to refresh his memory of his original concept, when needed. These rudimentary forms of visual records were the basis of further developing the concept of information sources. Since then man has recorded several events in different forms at different period of time. Each of the forms later became a source itself.

In olden days, only books, journals and newspapers constituted the sources of information. But today information has been recorded in various types of sources and the number and forms of sources are increasing in a rapid manner. Therefore, in the search for information, choice of the most appropriate source may make the difference between minutes on a task and spending hours or days, and sometimes even between success and failure.

Information service, therefore necessitates, knowledge of the different varieties of information sources, their scope, characteristics and uses

A source which transmits or embodies information is known as information source. Dennis Grogan has categorised the totality of the information sources in the universe broadly into two:

- Documentary sources
- Non-documentary sources.

DOCUMENTARY SOURCES

These are information sources that are available in the form of documents which are either printed, written or engraved materials that are intended for human communication. The documentary sources are again categorised on the basis of the level of organisation of information content as:

- Primary Sources
- Secondary Sources; and
- Tertiary Sources

PRIMARY SOURCES

Primary sources of information are the first published records of original research or new interpretation of an old theme or idea. These sources embody nascent, unfiltered original ideas. These sources are scattered and unorganised. The primary sources are the vehicles of new knowledge. These sources are useful to researchers to keep them abreast of the latest development in the field of research. This will also help the researchers to avoid duplication of research. A subject becomes a discipline in its own right when independent primary sources begin to be produced in that area. The rate of growth of a discipline to a large extent depends upon the amount of literature produced in the form of primary sources. Primary sources are published in a variety of forms such as:

- Periodicals
- Research reports
- Patents
- Standards
- Thesis and Dissertations
- Trade Literature
- Conference Proceedings ;and
- Government publications.

Periodicals

Periodicals include journals, bulletins, transactions or similar works which appear at regular period such as weekly, monthly, semi-monthly, quarterly in numbered sequence. According to Webster's Dictionary, a journal, often known as periodical, is a publication, dealing with matters of current interest ; often used as official or semi-official publications of special groups. The most of the primary sources of literature appears in the form of periodicals. The articles in periodicals report the results of recent research works and they are the main sources of research communication for the exchange of scientific information. Examples of periodicals are:

i) Economic and Political weekly. Mumbai, Sameeksha Trust. Weekly publication

ii) Nature. London, Macmillan. Weekly publication

iii) IALIC Bulletin. Calcutta, IASLIC. Quarterly publication

iv) Physics Fluids. New York American Institute of Physics. Monthly publication

Research Reports

Research reports are reports relating to research and development projects. Research reports generally give the results of R & D experiments or projects. They are primitive in the sense that they are published as and when research activities progress often, these are considered as primary sources of information. These are generally unpublished or semi-published literature. Examples. i) National Technical Information Centre Reports (NTIS);ii)Scientific and Technical Report, NASA,USA Patents.

Patents

Patent is an official document conferring an exclusive right, granted by a government to an inventor to manufacture, use or seek an invention for certain number of years; the list of such patents usually appear in the Government gazette. Patents are regarded as a part of primary sources because an invention has to be new, only then it can be patented. It may be mentioned that patents are of special interest to chemists and engineers. In each country, there is one publishing agency and these are serially numbered. In India, Indian patent office is responsible for granting patents. At present more than 4000 patents are granted every year. The patents are listed in bibliographical tools such as Indian Science Abstracts (New Delhi, NISCAIR); Chemical Abstracts (Eastern Pa, American Chemical Society) etc.

Standards

Standards are the publications issued by certain authorities such as International Standards Organisation (ISO), Bureau of Indian Standards(ISI) British Standard Institution(BSI) etc. It is something considered by an authority or by general consent as a basis of comparison. Standards ensure quality and reliability of the product. For industrial units and for design engineers, standards are important sources of information. A typical standard is a pamphlet containing definitions, methods, properties, measurements etc of the product. The types of standards are:

i) Quality & job performance standards;
ii) Determining standards;
iii) Weights and measure standards;
iv) Standard terminology;
v) Technical terminology standards;
vi) Value and practical standards; and
vii) Financial standards.

Examples : IS: 1553-195 Primary elements in the design of library building.

ISO/RY International code for abbreviations of title of periodicals.

Theses and Dissertations

Researchers who are pursuing M.Phil, Ph.D, D.litt, DSc etc in universities have to write a dissertation or thesis on a specific topic as partial fulfilment of the academic programme. These are usually expected to show evidence of original research, and are supposed to form an important category of primary sources for researchers in the concerned field.

Example : An investigation into the financial allocation in the Kerala, Cochin and Calicut university libraries during the plan periods (Ph.D thesis)

Trade Literature

Trade literature is an important source of information generated by commercial agencies. Trade literature aims to describe and also illustrate equipment or goods or processes or services relating to manufacturers. The basic objective of such a literature is to sell the products generated by the commercial agencies. It is published in various forms such as technical bulletin, price lists, data sheets etc.

Conference Proceedings

Any paper read or presented in conference organised at local, national or international, is a primary source of information. Papers presented in these conferences, give the light on new research and development. Conference literature can be divided into the following categories.

i) Pre-conference literature

ii) Literature presented in conference; and

iii) Post-conference literature.

Post conference literature is considered as conference proceedings.

Examples.: Proceedings of the national conference on Libraries in Distance education held at Kollam, Kerala Library Association,1988.

Proceedings of International Conference on Ranganathan's philosophy. New Delhi, Indian Library Association.

GOVERNMENT PUBLICATIONS

Quite a good number of publications are brought out by the local, State and Central Government. Publications such as Bills, Acts, Commission reports etc are considered as primary sources.

Examples : Dr.Radhakrishnan Commission Report on Higher Education,1948. Kothari Commission Report on Education, 1964.

UNPUBLISHED PRIMARY SOURCES

There are a number of information sources which remain unpublished under the category of primary sources. These are very useful information sources for researchers especially in social science subjects. They are:

- Company files
- Letters
- Memoranda
- Diaries
- Portraits
- Oral history
- Laboratory notebook
- Coins
- Archives
- Inscriptions on stones and tombs

SECONDARY SOURCES

Secondary sources are as the name suggests are derived from primary sources. They are generally organised and arranged according to a definite plan. Scattered units of information are collected and presented in a cogent manner. The secondary sources act as repositories of assimilated and digested data or information. They are usually called organised sources which act as keys to open primary information sources. The secondary sources are published in a variety of forms such as:

- Indexing periodicals
- Abstracting periodicals
- Review of progress
- Bibliographies
- Treatises
- Monographs
- Textbooks
- Translations
- Dictionaries
- Encyclopaedias
- Manuals
- Tables

Indexing Periodicals

An indexing periodical is a regularly issued compilation of titles of articles that appear in the current primary periodicals. An entry in an indexing periodical consists of information such as name of the author, title of the article, name of the journal, volume number, issue number, year and pagination.

Examples. Applied Science & Technology Index. New York, Wilson. Monthly. Indian Press Index. Delhi, Delhi Library Association. Monthly. Index India. Jaipur, Rajasthan University Library. Indian Science Index. New Delhi, NISCAIR. Annual.

ABSTRACTING PERIODICALS

An abstracting periodical is a regularly issued compilation of concise summaries of i) significant articles that appear in current primary source journals, and ii) of important new research monographs, reports, patents and other primary source publications in that field. It serves as an index, a tool for retrieval of information on a specific subject and provides survey of current state- of- the- art of the specific subject. The organisation of information in an entry of abstracting periodical consists of Citation and abstract.

Examples : Chemical Abstracts (CA). Eastern Pa, American Chemical Society. Weekly. Physics Abstract (PA) London, Institution of Electrical Engineers. Fortnightly. Biological Abstract (BA) Philadephia. Bioscience Information Services of Biological Abstracts. Semi monthly. Indian Science Abstract. New Delhi, NISCAIR. Library and Information Science Abstracts(LISA) Bowker Saur. Monthly.

Review of Progress

A review is a survey of the primary literature. It aims to digest and correlate the literature over a given period. It also indicates the developments and trends in the field concerned. It may appear as a collection of papers on regular basis or in the form of an article in a periodical. A review provides background information to a new problem in a suitable form and serves as a key to literature.

Examples : Annual Review of Information Science and technology. Washington DC, American Society for Information. Annual Publication.

Annual Review of Biochemistry. Palo Alto, Annual Reviews.

Bibliographies

A bibliography is an organised list of documents relating to a given subject or person. Subject bibliography, author bibliography, national bibliography, universal bibliography, trade bibliography, incunabula bibliography etc are various types of bibliographies.

Example. Bibliography on Superconductivity. William Shakespeare: A Bibliography. Indian national bibliography.

Treatises

A treatise is a comprehensive compilation or summary of information on a subject. A treatise on a subject provides enough information to a person to acquire basic knowledge, so essential for carrying out advanced research.

Example. Treatise on Inorganic Chemistry. New York, Elsevier.

Monographs

A separate systematic and complete treatise on a subject. Its limitation is up to only one subject and focus on latest and new information of the subject

Example. Prolegomena to library classification by Dr.S.Ranganathan.

Textbooks

This is a book written specifically for use of students, as part of their prescribed course of study. It is a main tool of teaching. It is not intended to impart in depth knowledge of a subject. A good text book takes into consideration the method of teaching and level of readership.

Example. Reference Service by Krishan Kumar

Translations

Translations are important secondary sources of information.

Their characteristics are the same as those of primary or secondary or tertiary sources from which these are translated.

Dictionaries

A dictionary contains the words of a language or the terms of a subject, profession or vocation arranged according to some definite order usually alphabetical one giving their meaning, pronunciation, spelling syllabification etc. Dictionaries can be categorised as General dictionaries, Subject dictionaries and Supplementary language books.

Examples. Oxford English dictionary. New York, Oxford University Press.

Webster's third new international dictionary of the English language. Merriam, Webster

McGraw-Hill dictionary of scientific and technical terms. New York, McGraw-Hill.

ALA Glossary of library terms with a selection of terms in related fields. Chicago, American Library Association.

Familiar quotations ed. by John Bartlett. Boston, Little Brown.

Roget's international thesaurus. New York, Crowell.

Encyclopaedias

An encyclopaedia is a compendium of knowledge. Knowledge is related to kind of readership, which an encyclopaedia intends to serve. Encyclopaedia can be categorised into General encyclopaedias and Specialised or subject encyclopaedias. A general encyclopaedia is a work containing articles giving essential general information on subjects in various branches of knowledge whereas specialised or subject encyclopaedia is a work containing articles giving information limited to a special field of knowledge.

Examples. New Encyclopaedia Britannica. Chicago, Encyclopaedia Britannica.

McGraw-Hill encyclopaedia of science and technology. New York, McGraw-Hill.

Manuals

A manual is an instruction book, which elucidates how to do something by means of specific and clear directions.

Examples. Manual for writers of term papers, theses and dissertations. Chicago, University of Chicago press.

Manual for the handling of applications for patents, dissertations and trademarks throughout the world.

Tables

Tables are convenient form to present data such as density, melting point, atomic weight, boiling points reactions etc. These are useful sources in science especially physical sciences and technology.

Example. International critical tables. New York, McGraw-Hill.

TERTIARY SOURCES

Tertiary sources are distilled out sources from primary and secondary information sources. The primary function of tertiary sources of information is to aid the searcher of information in the use of primary and secondary sources of information. Hence tertiary source is considered as key to open secondary and primary sources. The tertiary sources include the following types of information sources.

Bibliography of Bibliographies

A bibliography of bibliographies lists bibliographies which direct readers to useful bibliographies. It is otherwise known as Bibliographic Index. As the number of bibliographies published every year is large, bibliography of bibliographies are highly useful.

Examples. Index Bibliographicus. The Hague. FID Bibliographic. Index, cumulative bibliography of bibliographies. New York, Wilson.

Guides to Literature

A guide to literature assists a user to use literature of a specific subject. It helps to evaluate and introduce literature. It lays emphasis on literature rather than the content of a specific subject. It usually covers information pertaining to primary, secondary and tertiary sources on a specific subject.

Examples. Use of biological literature. London, Butterworths.

Guide to historical literature. New York, Macmillan

Directories

A directory is a list of names and addresses of persons, organisations, manufacturers or periodicals. It may list information in a way which best serves the requirements of its users so as to enable them to get the required information readily. There are various types of directories such as Industrial and business directories, and directories of specific scientific and technical organisation. They are local, national or international in scope.

Examples: World of Learning. London,Europa

Ulrich's International periodical Directory. New York, Bowker.

Yearbooks

Yearbook is published once in a year. It gives important events and developments in various subjects for the year concerned. The facts and figures relating to local, national and international events are arranged in a systematic order. Yearbooks are categorised into general yearbooks and subject yearbooks.

Examples. India: A reference annual. Delhi,. Ministry of Information & Broadcasting, publication division.

Manorama Yearbook. Kottayam. Manorama Publications.

Trend Reports

Trend report is an exposition of a subject, giving an account of the general direction of research and trends in the subject, based on a review of the documents on current developments.

Examples: Trend report on non-conventional energy. Trend report on nanotechnology

NON-DOCUMENTARY SOURCES

Non-documentary sources are otherwise known as 'paperless sources' These are information sources that are available not in the form of documents. Non-documentary sources are categorised into i)Formal sources or institutional sources ;and ii) Informal sources or human sources. Usually users think of documents as sources whenever they require information. But there are times when documents don't yield the necessary information. Then one has to look for other sources. This is where the non-documentary sources play a key role.

Formal or institutional sources include governmental organisations at the local, state or central levels, research and development organisations, industrial organisations, learned and professional societies and associations, academic institutions like universities, colleges, consultant organisations, information systems etc. While informal sources or human sources include colleagues in an organisation, subject experts or peer groups, information gatekeepers, guides, advisors, consultants, vendors, informal groups or 'invisible colleges' etc.

Information may also be transferred or exchanged in lecturers, discussions, seminars and conferences, get together open house exhibition etc. It may be worthwhile mentioning that a time, these non-documentary sources serve as pointers to the primary and secondary sources. Perhaps, these non-documentary sources are at times more convenient and easy as one can get directly information qua-information from the source, namely, the institutions and experts without taking the trouble of scanning and selecting the documents and retrieving from them the required information. Number of user studies pointed out that communication through non-documentary sources is very significant in scientific communication.

REFERENCES

Bonn, George S : Literature of Science and technology. In McGraw Hill

Encyclopaedia of Science and Technology. V7.New York, McGraw -Hill, 1971.

Grogan, Dennis: Science and Technology: An introduction to the literature. London, Clive Bingly, 1976.

Katz, WA: Introduction to reference work. New York, McGraw-Hill, 1982

Krishan Kumar: Reference service. Gaziabad, Vikas1981.

Chapter

3

Electronic Information Sources

Electronic Information Sources(EIS) may be defined as all those documents that are available in the electronic or digital form.The tools employed by traditional libraries, the environment and the whole concept of library services have undergone drastic changes owing to the advancements in the fields of information, communication and technology. Card catalogue which was reckoned as a convenient device for easy bibliographic search has become out dated when compared to the facilities offered by electronic applications. This scenario enjoins information skills training for both staff and readers and has drawn in a radical transformation within Library and Information system (LIS). From physical providers of information, libraries have become gateways to networked information providing access rather than holdings. A database, a structured collection of related data, is one of the most familiar types of EIS.

Electronic information sources offer vast opportunities for the readers. The information needed can be delivered from the most appropriate sources instantly and the user can sharpen his needs dynamically. Electronic information can therefore provide a number of advantages over traditional print based sources. Retrospective information search has become very effective. The data base can be accessed using combinations of keywords. They open up the possibility of searching multiple files at one time, a facility accomplished more easily than when using printed equivalents. The search results can be printed and searches saved for reference at a later date. They are updated more often than printed materials. One main advantage, especially to those with limited time to access the library, is their availability from outside the library by dial-up access. This underscores the importance of electronic resources which has to be integrated with the library systems

Magnetic tapes were introduced in the 1970s. But today electronic sources are available on CD-ROMS and on the internet. In the common parlance sources of information that are available on the internet are called online sources. These sources include E-journals, research publications, encyclopedia, dictionaries, atlases and the like. Internet, which was first developed in the USA in 1969, is the network of networks and is the largest computer network in the world. This global network currently consists of an estimated 14,000 networks, 100,000 hosts, and 20 million users world-wide. Thousands of journals and publications are now being made available in the Internet, thereby facilitating access to online journal articles and publications that are often free of charge. Likewise most of the libraries and databases in the developed countries are networked which greatly helps location and access of information. Libraries for that matter have become information gateways.

TYPES OF ELECTRONIC INFORMATION SOURCES

A brief discussion about the various types of electronic sources is given under.

E-Journals

Journal is a periodic publication appearing at regular intervals and continuously. It is the platform that carries the latest articles in various subject fields in science, technology and social sciences. Now many of the journals are available in the electronic form. Some of them are published in both paper form and in the electronic media. The latter are known as E-journals. These are also called virtual journals, or online journals. It is published in digital format and is available globally on the internet. Some of them may be in CD-ROM. "G Mc Millan defines E-journals as "any serials produced, published and distributed nationally and internationally via electronic network"

E-journals in CD-ROM are in physical form like books and can be acquired, stored and retrieved like a book. But it requires the necessary hardware and software to use it. But online journals on the Net can be used anywhere at any time. There is physical limitation for using it. There are a number of hosts like DIALOG that help to access the internet. There are several search engines that enable us to locate articles from the Net. One has to know the URL of the journal concerned. Electronic journals have helped publishers and scholars to disseminate information much more quickly.. The cost of acquisition of print form of journals is prohibitive and is enhanced frequently, but the cost of electronic format is much lower as the production and distribution costs are negligible. In the electronic version hypertexts can be provided which give linkages to the reader for referring related documents. It provides easy accessibility to all and selective dissemination of information is easier. The acquisition of infrastructure for using electronic database like the hardware and software is a bit costly. The absence of refereeing process in the case of electronic publishing is diluting the quality and authority of E-journal articles. The number of E-journals is on the increase. In July 1991 the number of E-journals was only 91, but in December 1997 it jumped to 2459.

E-Books

E-books have come to vogue recently. It is essentially the contents of a book distributed in the form of an electronic file. Theoretically any file that holds text can be called an E-Book. It is exactly like a book except that it remains in electronic form and not in hard form. It may be a single monograph or a multivolume set. They come in various formats. There are several programmes designed for reading it. They can be downloaded in pdf, html, plain text and rich text formats. They are also available in CD-ROM and floppy discs although the latter is now diminished in use. The use of personal computer is necessary for reading an e-book. An ideal E-Book should provide content of value, the ability to view online, the ability to download to a PC to view offline. The users should be guaranteed privacy for the content they access. Ideally it should also include embedded multimedia data, link to other electronic resources and should provide cross reference across multiple resources.

E-Books have been defines as an Electronic Version of a book by Webopedia. Jan O. Borchers defines E-Books as "An electronic book or E-Book is a portable hardware and software system that can display large quantities of readable textual information to the user and that lets the user navigate through this information" Anna Arias Terry defines E-Book as "an electronic concept originating from traditional books, reference material or magazines"

A common classification of E-Books is given by Don Hawkins. According to him there are four types of E_Books. They are:

Downloadable E-Books i.e. (i)Glassbooks and Guttenberg (ii) Dedicated E-Book readers like Gemstars,

REBs and Franklins E-Bookman. (iii) Print-on-demand books like Columbia university online book project (iv) We-accessible E-Books as on providers website and accessed on payment like the Springer E-Book collection.

Electronic books may be in any number of digital formats. There are a number of different formats and respective software applications to read them. There are book reading devices (other than personal computer) that display the contents of an electronic book and specialized software and hardware equipments are supplied along with it.

Well known publishers like the Oxford University Press, Princeton University Press and others have started e-publishing of books. This is big boon to publishers, authors as well as readers. Many websites allow readers to peruse the book and give their feedback on the work often directly to the authors. This is a great advantage over the print version. Electronic devices need less space and the electronic books are available through out the day. A single book reader containing several books can be carried around when you travel. The hyperlinks provided in the electronic format helps widen the scope of enquiry for a serious reader. The text size can be enlarged for those who have reading problems. It is ideal for archival and back up purposes. The electronic books are cheaper although the hardware devices are bit costly. Direct feedback can be given to the authors by the readers and thus the quality of the work can be improved. Self publication is a possibility that is not practicable in the case of hard copies. It cannot be lost, stolen, gone out of print or checked out from a library and copies may be printed in part or full. Now most of the newspapers are also available online. In brief the whole printed world is being replaced by electronic media and we are moving to an era of paperless society as predicted by FW Lancaster long ago.

The disadvantages are: i) the necessity of depending on a computer or an electronic device for displaying the electronic content. Ii) Regular supply of electric power is needed and in several countries power supply is not assured. iii) E-Books are given a low priority by many publishers at present. iv) Long exposure to computer screen can cause health problems. V) E-Book reading equipments are fragile and easily damageable vi) E-Books have security problems as computer piracy is now prevalent vii) In case of damage to the memory device, the whole book may be lost for ever. Hence backup devices are to be employed.

The major challenges faced in the acquisition and collection development of electronic resources are budget constraints, collection development strategies, E-Book standard and technology challenges, digital rights management software, cataloguing and metadata standards. There are also access challenges like cataloguing and indexing of E-documents, circulation problems of E-Books etc.

The electronic sources may be classified into 3 categories depending upon the organization of information content:

1. **Primary Sources:** These are nascent thoughts embodied in journal articles, theses and dissertations, patents, standards, research reports, Trade literature, conference proceedings, government publications like acts and bills and proceedings of parliaments and other legislative bodies, government reports etc.

2. **Secondary sources:** They are data bases like chemical abstracts, indexing and abstracting periodicals, reference books, encyclopedias, dictionaries, handbooks, translations, text books and the like.

3. **Tertiary sources:** These are bibliography of

bibliographies, guides to literature, yearbooks, directories, state of the art reports, trend reports, information digests, review articles etc.

INTERNET SOURCES

Internet is considered as the single biggest electronic information source. Some of the major Internet sources of information and databases are given below along with their site addresses.

1. AGORA (Access to Global Online Research in Agriculture (www.aginternetwork.org)
2. Free Medical Journals (http://www.freemedical journals.com)
3. Medical Journals and Books (*http://www.gfmer.ch/ MedicalJournals/Free medical.php*)
4. Medline/PubMed (http://www.ncbi.nlm.nih.gov)
5. The Oxford English Dictionary (www.oed.com)
6. Online Medical Dictionary ((www.graylab.ac.uk/omd/ index.html
7. Encarta online (www.microsoft.com/encarta/atlas/ atlas.htm)
8. Oxford Text Archive (http://info.ox.ac.uk/archive/ ota.html
9. Centre for Electronic Text in the Humanities (http:// etext.lib.virginia.edu/britpo.html)
10. Shakespeare Full text (telnet://lib.dartmouth.edu) CHEMDEX- Chemistry related Internet resources (http://www.shef.ac.uk/chem/chemdex)
11. Economics working papers Archive: (http:// econwpa.wustl.edu/wecome.html)

12. Internet Movie Database(http://uk.imdb.com)
13. Encyclopedia of Mythology (http://www.webcom.com/myth)
14. World city Maps (http://www.lib.utexax.edu/libs/PCL/Map-collection/map-collection.html)
15. Britanica online(http://www.ed.com)

There are several institutions providing electronic information to information seekers at large. Some of them are: Professional and Organizational Development Network in Higher Education, American Association of University Women, American Psychological Association, American Association of University Professors, Association of Universities and Colleges of Canada, and World Bank Social Indicators of Development.

LEGAL IMPLICATIONS OF ELECTRONIC PUBLICATIONS

The Digital Rights Management Systems (DRMS) is the most discussed legal issue related to E-Books. The DRMS is still in the evolutionary stage. It is related to both hardware and software aspects. Several aspects like intellectual property rights, limit by user, time, extent of contents etc. are debated vigorously by the experts. Although legal issues are involved in the case of E-Journals, the higher quantum of book content and the insistence of the publishers to impose controls make the matter all the more complicated. So they provide only limited usage rights for printing, downloading and copying. Inter-library loan and class room use is not allowed in the case of electronic publications. Publishers refuse to distribute their products in digital form to prevent piracy. Legal issues are pestering both readers as well as authors. An owner of a printed book may lend or sell it, but transactions are forbidden in the case of E-Books. This context is described by Howard Falk as 'Reader Restriction Software.'

There is tremendous cost advantage for E-Publications as there is no cost of printing, warehousing and distribution. Thus the financial risk for the publishers is very much reduced. Therefore Electronic publications are becoming more popular among librarians, publishers and the book industry as a whole. Hence, libraries should keep abreast with the developments in the electronic forms of publications. This will protect the interests of the reader community and the library profession as a whole. The full text capabilities of E-Publications should be integrated into all the library OPACs to enable the readers to obtain all the information they require. If we are not able to achieve this we may become obsolete. It will be quite relevant to quote Alvin Toffler who remarks 'Tomorrow's illiterate will not be the man who can't read; he will be the man who has not learned how to learn.'

REFERENCES

Borchers, Jan O. Electronic Books: definition, genres, and interaction design patterns. (http://readingonline.org).

Kumar, PSG: Information sources and services: Theory and practice. New Delhi, BR Publishing Corporation, 2004.

Chapter

4

Reference and Information Access Tools

We may define books into two categories. The first category is read continuously for the purpose of enjoyment, inspiration and information. These are ordinary books. The second category is those that are referred for consultation from time to time for getting specific information. These are called reference books. Since the role of these sources in reference and information access, they are now known as reference and information access tools.

Reference books vary from other books in several respects. A reference book is for consultation and ordinary books are meant for continuous reading. The biography of a person or a short story is a typical example for the latter. A reference book has the following characteristics.

1. It is used for consultation to obtain a particular peace of information. Some reference books like an encyclopedia provide information directly. But an indexing or abstracting volume just points to the source of information.

2. A reference book is not meant for continuous reading. No body reads a dictionary continuously.
3. A reference book lacks continuous exposition. It consists of disjointed information arranged alphabetically, chronologically or in some other helpful sequence.
4. Reference books are not lent out to members. It is meant for consultation within the library only.
5. A reference book is designed in such a manner that quick and effective reference is possible. An ordinary reader may need the help of the librarian to extract the required information from a reference book. They are published in various formats depending on the purpose and scope of the information contained.

CRITERIA FOR EVALUATION OF REFERENCE BOOKS

The following are the general norms or criteria for evaluating reference books.

1. Authority: The authoritativeness of a reference book is judged by the qualification, experience, expertise and reputation of the authors, editors, publishers, compilers and distributors.

2. Scope: It is the extent of treatment of the subject. We have to assess if the subject has been treated completely. No area of the subject should be omitted in the book.

3. Treatment: The treatment of the subject has to be reliable and exhaustive. Any omission is a serious drawback. It should include all facts and figures and description of the subject in question. The level of treatment of the subject is also considered here.

4. Arrangement: Depending upon the circumstances, the arrangement of subjects can be alphabetical, chronological, classified, geographical or any other manner. It should be helpful for easy retrieval of information and should be provided with an index for easy location of information.

5. Currency of Information: The information given should be up-to-date. Stale information is not useful and can mislead the readers.

6. Format: Format includes illustrations, maps, typeface, binding size etc. Illustrations and maps help to comprehensive the ideas better. Binding should be strong enough to withstand wear and tear. The quality of the paper should also be given due consideration..

7. Cost: The price of the item is an important consideration. A small library may not be able to afford to buy reference books of high prices. Similarly an important library may need a valuable set of reference books despite higher cost.

8. Special features like appendices and provision of up-to-date bibliographies are important points of evaluation. An index to the salient features treated in the book facilitates the search procedure.

9. Conclusion : It should include the overall judgment of the reference book

TYPES OF REFERENCE AND INFORMATION ACCESS TOOLS

The various types of reference and information access tools are discussed in the following sections.

Dictionaries

These are frequently used by all categories of readers. A language consists of numerous words. A dictionary provides the meaning, spelling pronunciation, accent, etymology and varied forms and usages of such words. Dictionaries are also known as glossary, thesaurus, lexicon etc. depending on the context and purpose of its compilation. Dictionaries which set authoritative standard for spelling, meaning pronunciation and usage are called prescriptive dictionaries. Samuel Johnson's Dictionary of the English Language (published in1765) is a prescriptive dictionary. The other kinds of dictionaries are just descriptive providing the meaning, spelling, pronunciation etc. Those who compile a dictionary are called lexicographers.

The main types of dictionaries are:

(1) General language dictionaries

(2) Subject dictionaries

(3) Dictionaries dealing with special features like synonyms and antonyms, quotations, abbreviations, technical words, dialects and slang and dictionaries for purposes of translation and that meant for members of certain professions. The description of words may be in the same language and alternate meanings in one or two languages may also be given. An English dictionary may thus describe the meaning in English only and may also give the Malayalam and Hindi equivalents of the word given. The latter are called bilingual dictionaries. Dictionaries are also available as trilingual (three languages), multilingual (more than three languages) or polyglot

Uses

The important uses of a dictionary are to find the meaning of words and phrases, to check spelling syllabification and hyphenation and the pronunciation of words, trace the etymology of a word, to find the foreign words used, to ascertain the dialects, to find out major place names and personal names etc.

The criteria for evaluating reference books enumerated above are applicable in the case of dictionaries. In addition to that the following considerations are important in evaluating dictionaries.

Vocabulary

The second important aspect in a dictionary is how exhaustive is the coverage and description of the words in a language. Certain unabridged dictionaries in the English language list nearly 300,000 words. An abridged one contains less words and description only. The type of dictionary chosen for a library depends on the need of the users. A village library may require an abridged version whereas a research library may need large ones.

Currency

The third aspect of importance in a dictionary is the currency of words. New words are added to all languages, more so in the case of the English Language where they liberally add words from other languages. Dictionaries should be updated by the publishers frequently. Computerization has facilitated the process of updating dictionaries.

Spelling

The fourth aspect is variations in spelling. The English language follows both the British and American spelling. The variant spelling of words should be clearly illustrated in a good dictionary.

Meanings

Different meanings of a word should be mentioned in a dictionary. A word may have different meanings in different contexts. This should be clearly illustrated in a dictionary.

Pronunciation

Pronunciation of words has to be indicated along with the word meaning.. In Malayalam and other Indian Languages words are pronounces as they are written. But this is not so in the case of Foreign Languages. Phonetic symbols are used to denote pronunciation in the English Language.

Etymology

Etymology gives the origin of words. In English a large number of words are taken from Latin, Greek, French and other languages. Etymology facilitates better comprehension of the meaning of words and its apt usage.

Grammar

Grammatical aspects like different parts of speech and usages are described in a good dictionary.

Synonyms

Synonyms of a word help to understand the context and usage in a better way. A good dictionary should give alternate terms for a word.

Syllabification

Syllabification demarcates the syllables in a word. This helps to understand the accents in a word and also in splitting a word at the end of a line.

The Physical Aspects

The physical make up like the calico used, the binding, printing quality etc. are important points. Hard bound copies of dictionaries should be preferred in order to withstand wear and tear caused by constant use.

Illustrations

Illustration is very important for comprehension. Any

amount of description of a Kangaroo can not give you an idea about it. But a picture of the animal gives one a perfect idea of it.

Special Features

Some dictionaries provide information on personalities, places, important historical events, list of abbreviations and other valuable information. This is an additional help to the readers.

Webster's Third New International Dictionary of the English Language. Springfield, Mass., Merriam Webster.

This was first published in 1909. Further editions appeared in 1934 and 1961. There is lot of variation between the second and third editions. The 1934 edition contained 600,000 words. But in 1961 the entries were reduced to 450,000. In the latter edition many obsolete words had been dropped. But, 100,000 entries including scientific and technical words were added. The dictionary provides spelling, syllabication, parts of speech, etymology, definitions, inflections, capitalization, illustrative quotations, pronunciation, labels (field, usage, geographic) and pictorial illustrations. The third edition contains few proper names or geographical names. For example there are no entries for Greece, Hercules etc. But the adjective forms of these proper nouns are included. In every five years a new edition is brought out. This is the oldest and most famous American dictionary having a wide coverage and without any sort of biases. In 1976 they brought out a supplement containing 6000 words that have been selected from science and technology, mathematics, music, politics, sports etc. Explanatory notes given in the beginning describe the different typefaces, abbreviations and other devices used that help in the effective use of the dictionary.

The Oxford English Dictionary Edition 2 by J A Simpson and E S C Weiner, Oxford, Clarendon Press 1989

The first edition of this dictionary was edited by James A H Murray, Henry Bradley, W A Craigie and C T Onions and came out in 1884. It had 10 volumes. It is known as Murray's Dictionary and included 414,825 words covering all the words known to the English Language since year 1150. The second edition came out in 1933 in 13 volumes.

Enormous quantity of work has gone into the completion of this work. Thousands of scholars have contributed to this prodigious dictionary.. The purpose of this dictionary is to trace history of English words highlighting differences in meaning, spelling, usage etc during different periods of time with quotations from 5000 authors of different ages. The twelve-volume *Oxford English Dictionary* and the single-volume Supplement represented the final statement from Oxford for many years to come. However, in 1957, Robert Burchfield was appointed as Editor for a new Supplement that would replace the 1933 volume and include much new information on the language. More scientific and technical terms were added, and the scope of the Dictionary was broadened to include considerably more words from North America, Australia, New Zealand, South Africa, South Asia, and the Caribbean. Substantially longer than the 1933 edition, this new Supplement was published in four volumes between 1972 and 1986.

In 1989 efforts were made to bring out a full, electronic text to form the basis of future revision and extension of the Dictionary. In Oxford John Simpson and Edmund Weiner with a core group of lexicographers reviewed, corrected, and edited this new electronic dictionary, as well as adding 5,000 new words. In all, the Project team succeeded in accomplishing around 85 per cent of its work by software, but the remaining 15 per cent required the critical eye of the editors. The culmination of this mammoth task was the setting in type and subsequent printing of the *Oxford English Dictionary*, Second Edition. In 1989 this was published on time, to great acclaim. The finished work, edited by Simpson and Weiner, fills 22,000 pages which are bound in twenty substantial volumes.

The *Oxford English Dictionary* on CD-ROM has been a great success. The electronic format has revolutionized the way people use the Dictionary to search and retrieve information. Complex investigations into word origins or quotations that would have been impossible to conduct using the print edition now take only a few seconds. Because the electronic format makes the *Oxford English Dictionary* so easy to use, its audience now embraces all kinds of interested readers beyond the confines of the scholarly community.

THESAURUS

Thesaurus literally means a treasure. In the case of books it is a treasure of words. In a thesaurus words carrying the same meaning and other related terms are listed and the nuances in meaning and usage are described. A thesaurus is to be evaluated in the same way as a dictionary. Roget's thesaurus of English Words and Phrases originally composed by B.Kirkpatrick and Webster's Collegiate Thesaurus by Merriam Webster are two well known English Language Thesauri. The entries are arranged in alphabetical order.

TECHNICAL DICTIONARIES

Special branches of knowledge and special occupations and professions use technical languages. For example Engineers, Space Scientists, and other professionals use several terms and usages unknown to ordinary people. Technical dictionaries compile and publish such terms for the benefit of the profession. Glossary of Chemical Terms edited by Hampel and G C Hawley and The ALA Glossary of Library and Information Science edited by Heartsill Young are two well known such dictionaries. Several classical works carry small glossary at the end.

DICTIONARIES OF QUOTATIONS

A dictionary of quotations is another type of dictionary. Quotations from eminent personalities are compiled and published. The quotation is cited and its author is mentioned subsequently. Some dictionaries classify the quotations according to the subject of the quotation. These dictionaries help people to select apt quotations for public speaking and citing in articles. The Oxford Dictionary of Quotations and Familiar Quotations by John Bartlet are well known dictionaries of quotations.

ENCYCLOPEDIAS

The Oxford English Dictionary defines an encyclopedia as "A literary work containing extensive information on all branches of knowledge usually arranged in alphabetical order." It is a comprehensive work that collects information from the whole universe of knowledge or from one or more subject areas, arranges it in alphabetic order and publishes them. People consider it as a ready source of reference for all their queries. The bibliographies given at the end of the articles guide readers for further reading. Large number of experts works in unison to bring out an encyclopedia. As the corpus of knowledge is growing incessantly, an encyclopedia has to be updated periodically.

The contributors and publishers of an encyclopedia should be well versed and reputed. Only then can their work be authoritative. The style of writing of an encyclopedia should be simple as it is meant for lay people. Children's encyclopedia should be easily comprehensible for them. The arrangement of topics in an encyclopedia is alphabetical. But a general index to the contents is essential since the articles refer to numerous events, names and facts. An encyclopedia should provide sufficient illustrations and maps wherever necessary. The binding and make up of an encyclopedia should be sturdy to withstand prolonged and constant use by readers. There are two types of encyclopedias viz general encyclopedia and subject encyclopadia.

Encyclopedia Britannica

Encyclopedia Britannica is one of the most popular general encyclopedias. The first edition of this encyclopedia was published during1768-1771 in Edinburgh. This was in three volumes. Several revised editions of this work were published from time to time. The ninth edition of this work appeared in 1889 and it was called the scholar's edition as it included long articles by learned men like Arnold Huxley, Swinburne and others. The publishers faced financial problems and the venue of its publication was shifted to the USA. The 1974 edition of this work was a thoroughly revised edition and was called as "two encyclopedias in one" It had 30 volumes and was divided into three parts.

1. Micropaedia: The Micropedia consists of 12 volumes containing about 60,000 short entries. This gives brief factual information. It performs the function of a ready reference tool. It contains references to detailed articles in Macropaedia on the same subject. Thus it performs as a reference and index tool.

2. Macropaedia: The Macropaedia has 17 volumes containing articles going deep into various subjects. It is meant for serious students. The articles are signed by reputed authors. Some articles are as detailed as a book, like the one on Western Literature consisting of 175 pages. The articles are appended with bibliographies. The absence of an index to the Macropedia is a serious drawback.

3. Propaedia: This is a single volume providing an outline and serving as a guide to the whole set. This was added due to the initiative of Mortimer J. Adler, the director of this edition. Broad subject heading are provided to outline human knowledge and shows relationship between ideas, persons and events. It is in fact an index to 15,000 entries in the other two parts. The outline of knowledge has been considered as a circle of knowledge without a beginning or end. The quality of the articles is very high. But certain ideologically biased radicals and unorthodox intellectuals are not included in the editorial board..

Britannica book of the year is brought out every year since 1938 and supplements the advancement of knowledge in every year. The 2010 edition of Encyclopedia Britannica is a very valuable reference work with 32 volumes.

Collier's Encyclopedia

Collier's Encyclopedia is published by P F Collier, New York. Originally it was published in 10 volumes. "Collier's New Encyclopedia" in 1921, 1926, 1928 wasedited by Francis J. Reynolds. After Collier's death in 1918, P.F. Collier & Son Company was bought by Crowell Publishing Company. In 1950 Crowell, Collier and Macmillan published the 20 volume Collier's Encyclopedia under the title Collier's Encyclopedia with Bibliography and Index. The preface describes as it "a scholarly, systematic, continuously revised summary of the knowledge that is most significant to mankind."It was expanded to 24 volumes in 1962. It was long considered one of the three major contemporary English-language general encyclopedias, together with Encyclopedia Americana and Encyclopedia Britanica.

The 1997 edition has 23,000 entries with few short

entries, as related subjects are usually consolidated into longer articles. A high percentage of the illustrations are in colour, and more full-colour illustrations had been added in recent years resulting in pictorial matter accounting for about two-fifths of the pages. Bibliographies are found in the last volume which also contains the 450,000 entry index. An annual Collier's Year Book was also published.

In 1998 Microsoft bought the rights to Collier's electronic version and incorporated it into its Encarta electronic encyclopedia. Atlas Editions (formerly Collier Newfield) retained the rights to publish the encyclopedia in book form. Since then, Collier's has ceased to be in print.

Collier's has a high place among the general encyclopedias. It has about 5000 authorities as editors, advisors and contributors. Most of the articles are signed and it has an international reputation. The articles are well designed and the subjects have been treated in a very lucid manner. William Katz opines that "Collier's Encyclopedia can be ranked good to excellent in almost all areas of evaluation."

McGraw-Hill Encyclopedia of Science and Technology

This was first published in 1960 and has been revised regularly. The latest edition is the tenth one that came out in 2007.This is a very popular and well-known subject encyclopedia and is widely used by all sections of the people. More than 1,700 new and updated articles appear in this edition. It has 20 volumes with 12,000 illustrations, 90 full-colour plates, numerous tables, and data appendices. There is a 500 page analytical index, an extensive topic index, and contributors list with Study Guides.

A tradition of excellence continues with the long-awaited tenth edition of McGraw-Hill's Encyclopedia of Science & Technology. This is a definitive source for keeping abreast with the amazing changes in science and technology with more than 1,700 new and updated articles and 12000 illustrations. There is a 500 page analytical index, an extensive topic index and study guides that helps to find information fast and with least difficulty.

Featuring entries written by international leaders in science and technology selected by McGraw-Hill's distinguished board of consulting editors, no other reference so thoroughly and dynamically chronicles the expanding frontiers, facts, and trends so vital to students, professionals, and general readers. There are 25 Nobel prize winners among the contributors. For more than four decades, McGraw-Hill's Encyclopedia of Science & Technology has provided readers with the information they need in an understandable, authoritative way. There is truly nothing else like it and no library can be called complete without a copy of this prestigious piece on its shelves.

There is a companion website that will provide selected updates to the Encyclopedia along with additional material such as special graphics and illustrations.

In many libraries, the McGraw-Hill Encyclopedia of Science and Technology is the first source patrons consult when beginning background research on a scientific topic. This is aimed at a non-specialist audience. The strengths of this encyclopedia are authoritative content written at a level accessible to the student or layperson and the specialists as well.

Encyclopedia of Library and Information Science, Encyclopedia of Mathematics, Encyclopedia of Religion and Encyclopedia of World Art are some other special encyclopedias.

There are some special aspects to be considered in evaluation an encyclopedia. Has the publisher done full justice to the purpose for which the encyclopedia had been originally intended? Allowance can be made for the limitation with regard to the subject. Another point is the bias of the publishers for certain ideologies or regions or philosophies. Knowledge is eternal and impartial truth. Index to the main text should be exhaustive and should not be parsimonious on cross references

YEARBOOKS AND ALMANACS

Yearbooks, as the term connotes is published annually on a particular theme around a country, the world in general, a particular pursuit or enterprise. All the developments in a particular year are narrated chronologically. Almanac was originally published to provide information on the movements of moon, low tide and high tides, calendar of holidays etc. Later almanacs started publishing annual data relating various aspects of human activities. Kats defines an almanac as "A compendium of useful data and statistics relating to countries, personalities, events, subjects and the like." Almanac and Yearbooks are now reckoned as identical as annual narratives. However almanacs include more retrospective material while yearbook lists the annual happenings occurring in the year reviewed. Some Yearbooks are supplements to certain encyclopedias like the Britannica Book of the year. Yearbooks are very helpful in finding information pertaining to events or developments in a particular year. Like other reference books, the authority, scope, currentness, arrangement, treatment, the provision of index and the format of the book are important considerations in evaluating a yearbook. Let us examine some important Yearbooks.

The Statesman Yearbook

This is a very popular yearbook published by Palgrave Macmillan Company. It got started by Thomas Carlyle with the help of William Gladstone. Their vision was to bring out an authoritative and accessible volume containing information essential for diplomats, politicians and the public in general. It is ranked as one of the top 20 best reference resources of the millennium. It is brought out every year without any interruption. A team of reputed contributors are working for it. A review of developments in all countries of the world is outlined. The important world events relating to the previous year is narrated in a nutshell in the beginning of the book. Statistical tables providing information on the economic social and cultural aspects of the nations of the world are also provided. The main text is divided into two parts. The first part gives information on the United Nations and its agencies, Intergovernmental agencies, the European Union etc. Details like the origins, functions, organization, the persons at the head of these institutions, publications of these institutions etc. are provided. In the second part, the countries of the world are listed alphabetically listed and detailed information about them is given. In case of large countries the details about the constituent states are also provided.

India: A Reference Annual

This is published by the Publications Division of the Govt. of India. It is a rich mine of information on India and the States and Union Territories and the economic, political and national life in general. This being an official publication of the Government of India, the information provided is authoritative and reliable. The data contained in there is authentic as they are collected from the government departments under the close scrutiny of the government officials. India 2010 is the latest edition. It covers a wide range of information on Indian economy, land and people, rural and urban development, industry and infrastructure, art and culture, flora and fauna, demographic details, geological structure, health, defense, mass communication, science and technology, education information technology, current affairs, sports, events of the past year etc. The latest edition gives details about the personnel working with the government of India, like members of parliament, various award winners. There is also an index at the end which gives a key to various entries given in the book.

The Europa World Yearbook, Whitaker's Almanac, World Almanac and Book of Facts, Universities Handbook, Malayala Manorama Yearbook, Kothari's Yearbook on Business and Industry etc. are also very useful yearbooks. The sub-organs of the United Nations publish a number of useful yearbooks, like UNESCO Statistical Yearbook, World Development Report, State of Food and Agriculture, U N Demographic yearbook etc.

DIRECTORIES

Directories provide information on people, organizations, addresses, places, telephone numbers etc. The Telephone Directory is a typical example of a directory. The ALA glossary of library terms defines directory as "A list of persons or organizations systematically arranged, usually in alphabetical or classified order, giving addresses, affiliations etc for individuals, officers ..." Directories are quick reference sources on persons, organizations, industrial units, places, dates of events etc. They are very easy to use. Government Directories, Institutional Directories, Trade and Business Directories, Professional Directories like "Who's Who" are the main types of directories. Some important and useful directories are discussed below.

A large number of queries of the readers can be answered with the help of directories. It is a easy access tool to meet ready reference queries.

World of Learning

The World of Learning was first published in1947 and has been revised regularly by Europa Publications. The present volume covers over 30,000 universities, colleges, schools of art and music, libraries, learned societies, research institutes, museums and art galleries. It provides details of more than 200,000 staff and officials and more than 550 international cultural, scientific and educational, organizations. It is completely revised and updated throughout the year. Professors at major universities are listed by name, together with the subjects in which they specialize. All entries provide name, address, telephone and fax numbers, e-mail and internet addresses of important office bearers of the organisation.

The online version of The Europa World of Learning provides a full range of sophisticated search and browse functions, and regular updates of content. The result is a site that offers an unprecedented level of access to global institutions of higher education and learning and to the people who are associated with them. This is a quick and easy to use source for information on academic institutions located around the world. It is well indexed and well edited. The online version complements the print edition and helps to browse and update frequently. The Times Literary Supplement describes it as the best single reference book on international scholarship.

Commonwealth Universities Yearbook

Association of Commonwealth Universities(ACU) is a voluntary organisation, which is registered in England and Wales as a charity and is controlled by its member institutions through an elected council. Her Majesty the Queen, the Head of the Commonwealth, is the Association's Patron.

Today's ACU combines the expertise and reputation of

over ninety years' experience with new and innovative programmes. Established in 1913, the Association of Commonwealth Universities (ACU) is the oldest inter-university network in the world. The ACU is designed to meet the needs of universities in the 21st century. Higher education is more international than ever before. At present the market for students and staff is a global one and research funds are increasingly allocated on an international, collaborative basis. Academic reputations are based on global connections. Innovation and good practice do not stop at national borders. There are five hundred members and they are spread across five continents and represent a diverse range of institutions. There are many similarities, like a common language, common values and similarities in their organization and management. Commonwealth universities are therefore able, through the ACU to network easily, extensively and fruitfully, sharing problems, solutions and good practice across a variety of higher education environments.

The Commonwealth Universities Yearbook was first published in 1914 under the title Yearbook of the Universities of the Empire. In 1948 the title changed to "Yearbook of the universities of the Commonwealth." Since 1958 it is published under the present title. It contains information about five hundred universities of the Common Wealth. Under each university or institution information is provided about year of foundation, the teaching staff and other officers, the teaching programmes, scholarships etc. In the country section there is a description of the universities in that country.

The main sequence of entries is by countries in alphabetical order followed by the name of the university. The latest edition is for the year 2008, a two volume set issued by Palgrave Macmillan. This is an invaluable source of information on university education.

Quantity and veracity of information, arrangement of facts, and quality of the publication are the special points of consideration in the selection of a directory. The Times of India Directory and Yearbook, Directory of Scientific Research Institutions in India etc are some other important directories. Many directories are now available in the online and this facilitates the efficiency of use and updating of information.

Up-to-datedness of information is an important aspect in evaluating a directory. In order to test the reliability of information one may take a few items from the directory and check them with other authoritative sources of information. By going through the preface, introduction and random scrutiny of the entries one can judge the overall quality of the publication.

HANDBOOKS AND MANUALS

Handbook is a compilation of information in a compact form for quick reference. A manual is an instruction book to guide a person to perform certain tasks. Both the terms are used synonymously. The Kerala Service Rules is a typical example of a manual. According to Louis Shores "Handbook is a reference book of miscellaneous facts and figures on one or many subjects assembled for ready use, in response to popular interest or to a specific need for concise, handy information." Handbooks and manuals are pointers to established knowledge and norms for procedure in a situation. Let us examine some of the important Handbooks.

Guiness World Records

Until 2000 it was known as The Guinness Book of Records and in previous U.S. editions as The Guinness Book of World Records. It is a reference book published annually containing a collection of world records. Both human achievements and the extremes of the natural world come under its purview. The book itself held a world record, as the best-selling copyrighted series of all-time. It is also one of the most stolen books from public libraries in the United States.

Reflecting on the history of this work is interesting. In May 1951, Sir Hugh Beaver, then the managing director of the Guinness Breweries, went on a shooting party by the River Slaney in County Wexford, Ireland. He became involved in an argument over which was the fastest game bird in Europe, the koshin, golden plover or the grouse. That evening at Castlebridge House he realized that it was impossible to confirm in reference books whether or not the golden plover was Europe's fastest game bird.

Beaver knew that there must be numerous other questions debated rightly in public in Britain and Ireland, but there was no book with which to settle arguments about records. He realised then that a book supplying the answers to this sort of a question might prove popular.

Beaver's idea became reality when Guinness employee Christopher Chataway recommended student twins Norris and Ross McWhirter, who had been running a fact-finding agency in London. The brothers were commissioned to compile what became The Guinness Book of Records in August 1954. One thousand copies were printed and given away.

After founding the Guinness Book of Records, the first 197 page edition was released in August 1955 and went to the top of the British bestseller lists by Christmas. "It was a marketing give away—it wasn't supposed to be a money maker," said Beaver. The following year it was launched in the U.S., and it sold 70,000 copies.

After the book became a surprise hit, many further

editions were printed, eventually settling into a pattern of one revision a year, published in October to coincide with Christmas sales. The McWhirters continued to publish it and related books for many years. On the TV series "Record Breakers", based upon the book, they would take questions posed by children in the audience on various world records, and would usually be able to give the correct answer. Ross McWhirter was assassinated by the Provisional Irish Republican Army in 1975. Following Roos McWhirter's assassination, the feature in the show where questions about records posed by children were answered was called "Norris on the Spot".

Sterling Publishing owned the rights to the Guinness book in the 1970s and under their management, the book became a household name in the USA. In 2006, Apax Partners purchased HiT entertainment which had the right to publication of Guinness Records and subsequently sold Guinness World Records in early 2008 to the Jim Pattison Group. With offices in New York and Tokyo, Guinness World Records global headquarters remain in London. Recent editions have focused on record feats by human competitors. Competitions range from obvious ones such as weight lifting to the longest eggs tossing etc. Besides records about competitions, it contains such facts as the heaviest tumor, the most poisonous plant, the shortest river, the longest-running drama in the USA etc. Each edition contains a selection of the large set of records in the Guinness database, and the criteria for that choice have changed over the years. The newest records are added, and the records that have been updated are added too. The Guinness Book of Records is the world's most sold copyrighted book, thus earning it an entry within its own pages.

Handbook of Chemistry and Physics

This handbook has been in existence since 1913. The Chemical Rubber Company in the USA is the publisher of the book. The CRC Press, LLC is a publishing group which specializes in producing technical books in a wide range of subjects. While many of their books relate to engineering science and mathematics, their scope also includes books on business and information technology. It is also well known for its wide range of books on forensics. CRC Press is now a subsidiary of Informa. The CRC Press was originally founded as the Chemical Rubber Company (CRC), which supplied laboratory equipment to chemists. In 1913 the CRC offered a short manual called the Rubber Handbook as an incentive to purchase one of their products. Since then the Rubber Handbook has evolved into the CRC's flagship book, the CRC Handbook of Chemistry and Physics. In 1973, in light of the success of its publishing ventures, the company changed its name to CRC Press, Inc, and exited the manufacturing business. In 1986 it was bought by the Times Mirror Company. In 1997-98 it became a publicly held company. In 2003 CRC became part of Taylor and Francis Publishers, which in 2004 became part of the UK publisher Informa. The content of the ninetieth edition, 2009-2010, of the CRC Handbook of Chemistry and Physics is now available online.

Helpful presentation of facts and uptodateness of information given are additional evaluation criteria in the selection of handbooks and manuals.

The McGraw-Hill Computer Handbook and Handbook of Monetary Statistics of India by RBI, Limca Book of Records are some other useful handbooks for a library. Guerrilla warfare handbooks and manuals, Torture handbooks and manuals, U.S. Army and CIA Interrogation, self help books etc. are some of the very special kinds of handbooks.

STATISTICAL INFORMATION SOURCES

The collection, storage, classification and analytical interpretation of numerical facts i.e. data are important in scientific research, government administration and in every sphere of human enterprise. Government's policy matters are decided by the results of statistical analysis. The administrators will be groping in darkness in the absence of data in their day today decisions. Various government agencies and organizations are the agents collecting primary statistical data. International agencies like the UN and its subsidiaries also collect large quantity of data from various spheres of activity. National governments report this data to these agencies. Secondary statistical data appears in books and reference materials released by publishers that are quoted from original data sources. Statistical data analysis has limitation as systematic collection of data started only in the19th century and hence comparative study prior to this period is not possible. Huge mass of data takes time to analyze even in this age of computerization. Sometimes the authenticity of the data itself is held in question. A reference librarian should have sufficient awareness and develop special skills to meet the statistical queries from the readers.

International Trade Statistics Yearbook

This is published since1950 by the United Nations Statistical Office. The *2008 International Trade Statistics Yearbook* is new and different from previous editions as it has been re-designed and its two volumes are published separately. Volume 1 is *Trade by country* and has been compiled early in 2009 to allow for an advanced release of an overview of international merchandise trade in 2008. Volume II contains detailed tables showing international trade for individual commodities and eleven world trade tables covering trade values and indices. This has been compiled in December 2009 approximately six months after the submission of Volume I. Overall, data for a total of 258 commodities are shown in Volume II. The information for 2008 is based on data provided by 139 countries (areas), representing 95% of world trade of 2008.

The presentation of the information on individual commodity has been re-designed. Instead of detailed tables, now so called commodity trade profiles show an analytical and condensed view of the evolution of trade in a particular commodity by using graphs, overview tables and descriptive text.

The Trade Statistics Branch (TSB) of the United Nations Statistics Division is responsible for International Merchandise Trade Statistics (IMTS) and Statistics of International Trade in Services (SITS). Additional activities include Tourism Statistics, Distributive Trade Statistics (DTS) and the Compilation of Basic Economic Statistics.

For each of these statistical areas TSB develops or is involved in the development of the international methodology and cooperates with countries and international organizations to strengthen statistical capacity. For merchandise trade (IMTS) and trade in services (SITS) TSB collects and disseminates detailed data. The Statistics Division is committed to the advancement of the global statistical system. They compile and disseminate global statistical information, develop standards and norms for statistical activities, and support countries' efforts to strengthen their national statistical systems. TSB facilitates the coordination of international statistical activities and support the functioning of the UN Statistical Commission as the apex entity of the global statistical system.

Census of India Reports

A census is the procedure of systematically acquiring and recording information about the members of a given population. It is a regularly occurring and official count of a particular population. The term is used mostly in connection with national population and door-to-door censuses to be taken every 10 years according to United Nations recommendation. The term "census" comes from Latin language and it literally means counting. The history of census can be traced to the Roman Empire where they used to take enumeration of the population within their country with the intention of collecting taxes and recruiting soldiers. The Census data is commonly used for administration, research, determining the number social and religious groups, business marketing, and planning as well as a base for sample surveys.

The census of India reports are important massive statistical information source about India. It is undertaken once in ten years. The first census was conducted in 1872 by the then British Government and the second one was conducted in the year 1881 and thereafter it has been done consistently without any break. The last census in India was completed in 2001. Statistical and descriptive reports issued by the Central and State Governments are very authoritative documents. The district census handbooks, village and town directories also contain very valuable information.

The census reports are divided into 10 parts. Part 1 covers general reports, Part 2 census tables on population, Part 3 establishment reports, part 4 housing report and tables, part 5 special tables and notes on scheduled castes and scheduled tribes, part 6 town and village directory, part 7 special report on graduate and technical personnel, part 8 administrative reports, part 9 census atlas and part 10 district census handbooks, miscellaneous report and tables.

The numerous tables, and maps and factual information published in the census reports are valuable sources of information. The enumerators collect the data very carefully and it is quite reliable. There is considerable delay in publishing the census reports, which is unavoidable. The census of India, in addition to statistics related to the Indian Population provides also extensive information on social, cultural, religious, housing, administrative and geographic information related to the country, the people and the government in general. The information is original and authentic and is an asset to any library. The Census reports are good source of information for meeting the reference queries of the readers.

UN Demographic Yearbook, UNESCO Statistical Yearbook, Statistical abstract of the United States, Statistical Abstract India, RBI Bulletin, National sample survey reports(CSO),India Labour Statistics etc are some very useful statistical reference sources.

GEOGRAPHICAL INFORMATION SOURCES

Geographical queries are often raised by readers. These relate to the physical geography, political geography, economic geography, climate related geography, transportation geography and the like. Geographic information is provided by maps and atlases, gazetteers, geographic guides and the Online Geographic Information System.

Maps and globes are miniature representation of earth and its territories. Maps are only two dimensional, but globes are spherical. It is a replica of the earth and represents the earth in relation to all its physical features. In schools especially globes are very essential to demonstrate the movements of the earth vis-à-vis other celestial bodies. They help us to locate different places and other physical, geographic, climatic and political aspects of different parts of the world. An atlas is a collection of maps of different regions or countries that are arranged in a helpful sequence.

Atlases contain explanatory notes which can further elucidate geographic facts in detail. An atlas also provides an exhaustive index to the information given in the maps and helps quick reference.

A gazetteer is a geographical dictionary or directory, an important reference for information about places and place names, used in conjunction with a map or a full atlas It typically contains information concerning the geographical makeup of a country, region, or continent as well as the social statistics and physical features, such as mountains, waterways, roads etc.. Examples of information provided by gazetteers include the location of places, dimensions of physical features, population, economic growth, literacy etc. This information is generally divided into overhead topics with entries listed in alphabetical order.

Gazetteers existed in Greece since the ancient times. The first known gazetteer of China appeared with the age of print media by the ninth century. Although existent only in fragments, the geographer Stephanus of Byzantium wrote a geographical dictionary in the 6th century which influenced later European compilers of gazetteers by the 16th century.

Gazetteers give a detailed treatise on different places and regions and are often arranged in the alphabetical order of their names. Gazetteers are also called geographic dictionaries and help to locate countries, towns, villages, mountains, lakes, monuments etc. Gazetteers give detailed information and are a very good geographical information source in a library. Webster's New Geographical Dictionary, Chambers World Gazetteer, Gazetteer of India published by the Ministry of Information and Broadcasting are very valuable gazetteers.

The Times Atlas of the World

According to William Katz this is the best single volume

atlas available. He further adds that no American atlas is a match to this British Atlas. The first version of The Times Atlas of the World appeared as The Times Atlas in 1895; more printings followed up to 1900. It was published at the office of The Times Newspaper in London and contained 117 pages of maps with an alphabetical index of 130,000 names. The atlas was a reprint of Universal Atlas of Cassell & Co. published in 1893.

The second generation of the atlas was issued in 1920 as The Times Survey Atlas of the World and was prepared at the Edinburgh Geographical Institute under the direction of famous John George Barholomew. It contained 112 double page maps with 200,000 names.

In 1967, an edition in one volume in which the maps were printed back to back was published as The Times Atlas of the World. Comprehensive Edition with 123 leaves of maps is the 9th edition of 1992. This edition also appeared in a German, a Dutch and a French translation. Some discoveries by satellite surveys were also included.

The 10th or "Millennium" edition came out in 1999. In contrast to its predecessors, it is completely produced by means of computer-cartography.

The New International Atlas

This was first published in 1969 by Rand McNally and Company, Chicago. William Katz rates this as the second choice of atlases after Times Atlas of the World. An excellent team of cartographers have brought out this atlas. The Rand McNally New International World Atlas is a medium format World Atlas. Although the page size is smaller than the Times Atlas Comprehensive Edition and the National Geographic World Atlas, it makes up for this by having 287 map pages and an index of 177,000 place names.

The Rand McNally Atlas covers most of the World at either 1:6,000,000 or 1:3,000,000 with extremely attractive and detailed physical maps which rival the 1:5,000,000 and 1:2,500,000 maps of the Times Atlas. Unlike the Times Atlas, it also has the best selection of 1:1,000,000 and 1,300,000 urban area maps. As would be expected from an American publisher, the maps of North and Central America are second to none, but the rest of the world is also very well mapped, apart from Siberia and Northern Canada. Anyone looking for an alternative or complementary World Atlas to the Times Atlas Comprehensive Edition, especially for urban mapping, need look no further than the Rand McNally New Universal World Atlas. The index of this atlas contains 160,000 entries of place names (including 35,800 US names) arranged in alphabetical order.

The authority of the publishers is very important. The National Geographic Society, C.S.Hammond and Co. and The Oxford University Press are some of the renowned geography publishers. The Survey of India is the government authority responsible for the issue of official maps in India. Guides are brief descriptions of places or regions and give minute details about cities, hotels, tourist sites and historic monuments etc.

Handbook for Travelers in India, Pakistan, Burma and Ceylon and The Traveler's Handbook are important sources in this respect. The India Handbook published by Trade and Travel is a comprehensive and very useful travel guide on India

Gazetteer of India: Indian Union

This was first published as Imperial Gazetteer of India in 1881 in 9 volumes on the proposal of W W Hunter. Its second edition was published in 14 volumes during 1885-1887, the third edition in 1907-1909 comprising of 26 volumes. The Imperial Gazetteer of India is a historical reference book about India. It was first published in 1881. Sir William Wilson Hunter made the original plans of the book, starting in 1869.

The 1931 edition had four volumes covering the geography, history, economics and administration of India, 20 volumes of the alphabetically arranged gazetteer listing place names and giving statistics and summary information and one volume each comprising the index and atlas. Besides, district gazetteers are also published. Their total number is going to be over 300 and is brought out by the State Governments. Bibliographies are provided for further reading. Numerous tables, charts, maps etc. are also provided. Herculean effort has been put into the compilation of this work. This gives invaluable information for administrators and the people at large. It is an asset for any library.

Evaluation of maps and atlases is somewhat different. It requires special knowledge in order to evaluate maps. Date is an important consideration, as place names and division or merger of nations take place. For example Bangladesh was not in existence before 1971. The use of scales and special colouring of territories are also important considerations.

BIOGRAPHICAL INFORMATION SOURCES

The exemplary life of great personalities who have made valuable contributions to humanity is certainly worthy of emulation. Their life career should be recorded and made available to future generations. This is the raison de'etre for biographic information sources in a library. Louis Shores has defined biographical dictionary "As essentially a directory of notable persons, usually arranged alphabetically by surnames, with biographical identifications that range from brief outline to extended objective as possible." The purpose of a biographical dictionary is to provide information and also to find out eminent personalities in various professions. The national sentiments also compel one to compile biographic information of leading personalities of a nation. A biographical dictionary is the best source to provide this information. Biographical information is also available in encyclopedias, almanacs and other reference sources.

International Who's Who

Published annually since 1935, the International Who's Who 2010 is now in its seventy-third edition. This is edited by Europa Publications and published by Routledge, Providing hard-to-find biographical details for over 22,000 of the world's most prominent and influential personalities, this outstanding reference work records the lives and achievements of men and women from almost every profession and activity..

The editorial team aims to include all those who have raised to the top of their field or profession - from the headline makers to the unsung experts whose achievements and talents guarantee their inclusion. Entries are taken from across the world and from a broad sweep of professions, to include the leading figures from the worlds of science, medicine, business, finance, politics, international affairs, diplomacy, law, art, music, entertainment and fashion, to name but a few. There is also a separate section that details reigning royal families.

The comprehensive, newly-expanded **World Who's who** brings together current and hard-to-find biographical information on almost 60,000 of the most gifted, famous and influential men and women in all fields.

Using a full range of sophisticated search and browse functions in **World Who's Who**, researchers can quickly find the current career, contact and other biographical details that they need on their most eminent contemporaries. Heads of state, ministers, politicians, diplomats and religious leaders, the famous and successful in business, finance, technology, film, music, literature, fashion, sport and a host of other professions have been carefully selected by the Europa Biographical Reference team of editors.

Dictionary of National Biography

Dictionary of National Biography is edited by S.P.Sen, Institute of Historical Studies, Calcutta.. There are 350 contributors who are well-known scholars or research fellows. This is a four volume book published during 1972-1974. It aims to cover eminent personalities from politics education, journalism literature, science, business and industry and other walks of life. Persons who have made contributions in the regional level are also included. The whole of undivided India before independence comes under the coverage of the work. The work covers 1400 biographies. The entries are arranged alphabetically by surname according to their English spellings. The descriptions are short essays of varying length. Indian language source materials have been given preference in collecting facts about the persons of Indian origin. The essays are not merely concerned with what a man did, but also what he thought and how he felt vis-à-vis the different problems of life and society. At the end of each entry the name of the contributor and the name of research personnel who gathered the information are also given.. This is a standard reference book authentic and factual and is useful for scholars as well as the general public.

Guidelines for inclusion of a name in a biographical dictionary should be clearly defined. The readers for whom the work is addressed is another important consideration. The length of entry, frequency of revision, method of compilation, arrangement of the contents, additional norms of evaluation of biographical reference books etc to be considered.

Merriam Webster's Biographical Dictionary, the Dictionary of National Biography (OUP), Who's Who in America, Dictionary of Scientific Biography, N. York, McGraw-Hill, Modern Men of Science and Current Biography (H W Wilson) are some of the renowned biographical information sources. National Biographical Dictionary of India (Delhi, Sterling), and Times of India Directory and Yearbook including Who's Who 1914 (Times of India Press) are some of the biographical reference sources about India. There are also biographical dictionaries of personalities in different persuasions like Science and Technology, Literature, Social Sciences, History etc.

Revision and updating of biographical sources are an important consideration in evaluating a biographical reference source. A librarian should give special care in evaluating a biographical information source.

INDEXING AND ABSTRACTING PERIODICALS

There are three types of indexes. General indexes are those covering several topics contained in different articles. The Guide to Indian Periodical Literature is an example for this. The second type is Subject Indexes and is compiled on a specific subject from a vast base of journals and other publications. Applied Science and Technology Index is an example for this. The third type is an index to a single periodical. Several journals issue indexes covering the back runs for the benefit of their readers. Some newspapers like the Hindu, New York Times etc. publishes indexes. There are also indexes on serial publications released by governments. An American Librarian, William Frederick Poole was one of the pioneers in compiling index called Poole's Index to Periodical Literature. Guide to Indian Periodical Literature:

Social Sciences and Humanities, Applied Science and Technology Index, Agrindex (FAO), Index Medicus, Current Contents etc. are some other valuable indexes. These help to find information from a wide variety of applied science specialties like neural networks to nuclear engineering, leading trade and industrial journals, professional and technical society journals, specialized subject periodicals, buyers' guides, directories, and conference proceedings.

Let us examine some of the indexing periodicals in detail.

Applied Science and Technology Index

This Indexing was called Industrial Arts Index during 1913-1957 and was issued as a monthly by the H W Wilson Company, New York. In 1958 it was split into Applied Science and Technology Index and Business Periodicals Index. It is a bibliographic database that indexes articles of at least one column in length. English-language periodicals published in the United States and elsewhere are covered. Non-English language articles are included if English abstracts are provided. Periodical coverage includes trade and industrial publications, journals issued by professional and technical societies, and specialized subject periodicals as well as special issues such as buyers' guides, directories, and conference proceedings. Up-to-date subject headings keep pace with scientific and technical developments. Charts, graphs, illustrations, and PDF page images, make technical information easy to understand. A wide variety of science and technology subjects like Acoustics, Aeronautics, Artificial Intelligence, Environmental Engineering, Nuclear Engineering, Space Science, Waste Management etc. are covered by the index. Abstracts and indexing of nearly 800 periodicals as far back as 1983 and full text of articles from more than 200 journals since 1997 are available. Students, educators, and other researchers will use this resource to find accurate, balanced information in the sphere of Science and Technology.

Applied Science and Technology Index Retrospective 1913-1983 provide contents from the acclaimed Applied Science & Technology Index. Book reviews are arranged by author in alphabetical order in a separate section. Extensive cross references guide the readers without any confusion. Timeliness in providing information is maintained as this is brought out every month without fail except in July. This is the perfect reference for tracking down important studies, exploring historical controversies. As this is one of the major indexing service in science and technology it should be treated as an essential document in a major library. Many of these indexes are now in the machine readable format and can be easily used.

Index Medicus

Index Medicus is published by the National Library of Medicine (NLM) at Bethesda, Maryland State in USA. It is a relational database of the United States National Library of Medicine for the storage and retrieval of Medical Literature. It was initiated by John Shaw Billings, head of the Library of the Surgeon General's Office. This library later evolved into the United Publication in 1879 and continued monthly through 1926, with a hiatus between 1899 and 1902. During this hiatus, a similar index, the Bibliographia Medica, was published in French by the Institut de Bibliographie in Paris. The Index Medicus was amalgamated with the American Medical Association's Quarterly Cumulative Index as the Quarterly Cumulative Index Medicus in 1927. The American Medical association continued to publish this until 1956. From 1960 to 2004 the printed edition was published by the National Library of Medicine under the name Index Medicus/

Cumulated Index Medicus (IM/CIM). In May 1962, accompanied by armed Pinkerton guards, the collection was moved from Cleveland to the Library's current location in Bethesda, Maryland.

An abridged version was published from 1970 to 1997 as the Abridged Index Medicus. The abridged edition lives on as a subset of the journals covered by "'Pubmed 'or "core clinical journals." The last issue of Index Medicus was published in December 2004 (Volume 45). The stated reason for discontinuing the printed publication was that online resources had supplanted it, most especially PubMed, which continues to include the Index as a subset of the journals it covers.

Selection of journal into the Index is not automatic and depends on a journal's scientific policy and scientific quality. These criteria are evaluated by the "Literature Selection Technical Review Committee" and the final decision is made by the NLM director. The review process may include outside reviewers and journals may also be dropped from inclusion. Each article included in the Index Medicus is given as many subject headings as required. The subject Headings are selected from a controlled vocabulary called Medical Subject Headings (MeSH) which is published and revised annually as part two of the January issue of the Index Medicus. The latest information on biomedical subjects is selected to keep abreast with the mainstream of development.

The National Library of Medicine provided computer based system for biomedical reference storage and retrieval with the development of Medical Literature Analysis and Retrieval System (MEDLARS) since January 1964. This helped to improve the quality of Index Medicus and to allow fast searching of the large computer store of references.

The online bibliographic retrieval system known as

MEDLINE (MEDLARS Online) was initiated in October 1971. Medline is a pioneering online bibliographic database containing more than 70, 00000 citation from 3500 recent medical periodicals from 70 countries. During 2005-2009 a total of 3,219,081 citations were added to Medline.

About 30,000 citations are added to the basic database every month. Medline incorporates all of Index Medicus, Index to Dental Literature and International Nursing Index covering research practice, administration, policy issues, health care service, dental research and nursing information.

Now MEDLINE is also available on CD-ROM which is a big boon to Index Medicus users world-wide. The National Medical Library of India provides this indexing service on CD-ROM in India.

Index Medicus is considered as an excellent and indispensable indexing service for students and faculty in and allied subjects. It has become renowned and accessible to the entire world by its online and CD-ROM services.

Science Citation Index and Social Science Citation from Institute of Scientific Information, Philadelphia, Business Index from California Social Sciences Index by H W Wilson Company, Indian Press Index by Delhi Library Association are some other well known indexing journals.

Coverage of journals, cross references, and depth of indexing, items of information provided with an entry, currency and timeliness, right selection of subject headings, periodic cumulating of index, etc. are some of the additional features one observes when evaluating this index.

ABSTRACTING JOURNALS

Denis de Sallo published the first journal, Journal des Scavans in French on 5th January 1665. This was followed by the publication of Philosophical Ttransactions published from London on 6th March, 1665.

The period following the Second World War has witnessed a massive growth of knowledge and a corresponding increase in journal articles, reports, theses, seminar papers etc. This is the result of increasing research activities in science and technology and social sciences and consequent ramification of new subjects. The Ulrich's International Periodical Directory of 2003 lists 260, 500 periodicals. It is reckoned that the literature in science and technology doubles in a short span of 8yeras. The readers as well as the librarians are embarrassed at this gigantic growth in literature and find it helpless to dig out information from this heap. Abstracting of these articles into short summaries helps the readers to easily locate and evaluate an article. According to William A Katz abstract offers an objective analysis of what a given article, book, film etc. contain.

An abstract alerts a reader to the summary of articles scattered in a vast ocean of journals. It saves his time by enabling him to read through the abstracts.. An abstract is often "the terse presentation in the author's own language of all the points made in the same order as in the original piece of primary document that may be a book, a journal article, as speech, conference proceedings etc. It is the summary of the document representing the quintessence of its contents. Since abstracts are repository of summaries retrospective retrieval of information becomes easy. It serves as an encyclopedia of journal articles.

There are indicative abstracts and informative abstracts. Indicative abstracts are just brief summary mentioning what the article deals with. Informative abstracts are longer and present the essential data and conclusions. It describes the main contents of the article and a reader can make a true evaluation of the article without reading it through. An informative abstract usually summarizes the scope, the data and facts, the analysis and conclusions and interpretations of the order. Informative abstracts are more helpful and popular among the user community. Specialists always prefer informative abstract The length of an abstract is between 50 to 150 words.

In addition to the above types there are three other types. The first one is discipline oriented abstract. These abstracts are prepared for abstracting services for a particular branch of knowledge. The second one called slanted abstracts which emphasizes on the subject oriented part of the document. These are meant to serve the specific requirements of an organization. The third one is the mission-oriented abstracts that are prepared for an abstracting service concerned with the application of specific branch of knowledge like engineering abstracts.

It often requires considerable time in preparation and publication of indexing journals. The computerized databases have helped to solve this problem to a great extent. The authority of the publishers, scope and coverage, arrangement of the entries- either alphabetically or classified, the items of information provided under each entry, the frequency and currency of publication, provision of index and the format of the book are important consideration in evaluating an indexing journal. Brevity, clarity and accuracy are important hallmarks of an indexing journal. Biological Abstracts (BIOSIS), Chemical Abstracts (American Chemical Society), Excerpta Medica (Elsvier Science), Historical Abstracts (American Bibliographical Centre), Library and Information Science Abstracts (Bowker-Saur), Dissertation Abstract International (Michigan University) etc. are some of the leading abstracting journals.

Uses of Abstracting Journals

It alerts a reader to newly published articles scattered in a wide ocean of literature. It obviates the actual perusal of the article by providing summary of the document and saves the precious time of the reader. Abstracting journals being summary of the documents is a repository for information retrieval. It has an encyclopedic function. The ASLIB observes: "The index of an appropriate abstracting journal should be used whenever information is being sought on any subject and it is likely to lead to information of more value than would be obtained from any other books of reference." Classified abstracts bring together material on the same subject which may be scattered in a vast ocean of literature. Abstracts remove the language barrier by giving a summary of the contents of the document in a language not known to the reader. An informative abstract is often considered as a substitute for the original document.

Let us examine some of the leading abstracting journals.

Chemical Abstracts

This is published from Columbus in Ohio by the American Chemical Society. Chemical Abstracts began as a volunteer effort and developed from there. The use of volunteer abstractors was phased out in 1994. Chemical Abstracts has been associated with the American Chemical Society in one way or another since 1907. For many years, beginning in 1909, the offices of Chemical Abstracts were housed in various places on the campus of Ohio State University. In 1965, CAS moved to a new 50 acre site just north of the Ohio State campus. In 1907, William A. Noyes was the first editor of the new publication, Chemical Abstracts.

Chemical abstracts contain English language abstracts and indexes of world's literature of chemistry and chemical engineering. Approximately 8,000 journals, technical reports, dissertations, conference proceedings and new books in 50 languages, are monitored yearly, as are patent specifications from 27 countries and two international organizations. Chemical Abstracts ceased print publication on January 1, 2010 and is now available online.

Indian Science Abstracts

The international abstracting services bear a bias for the English Language speaking nations and developed countries in general. Hence this is a very useful source providing bibliographic control of Indian scientific literature. This was originally published by the Indian National Scientific Documentation Centre (INSDOC) which collects and documents information in different fields of science and technology. It was established in 1952 and is based at Sansad Marg in New Delhi. In 2002 it merged with the National Institute of Science Communication (NISCOM) and is now known as National Institute of Science Communication and Information Resources (NISCAIR). Both NISCOM and INSDOC, the two premier institutes of the Council of Scientific and Industrial Research (CSIR), were devoted to dissemination and documentation of Science and Technology information. Broadly the core activity of NISCAIR will be to collect/store, publish and disseminate science and technology information through a mix of traditional and modern means, which will benefit different segments of society.

Indian Science Abstracts (ISA) is a semi-monthly abstracting journal which has been reporting scientific work done in India since 1965. Original research articles short communications, review articles, and informative articles published in current scientific and technical periodicals, proceedings of conferences and symposia, monographs and other publications, as well as patents, standards and theses are reported in ISA. ISA is now available online.

The major research and development programs are design and development of science and technology databases, network-based online services, research and development in information science and technology, foreign language translations, and human resource development in information science and technology.

The information is given in classified sequence, each entry providing information about the author including the address of the first author, title and all relevant bibliographic information. Titles in foreign languages are translated into English and the language of the original article is indicated.

Scope and Coverage

Indian Science abstracts includes over 1000 Indian scientific periodicals while it scans about 2000 foreign scientific periodicals for preparing about 36,000 abstracts per annum in twenty four issues. It includes abstracts of original articles, reviews, short communications published in periodicals, Conference proceedings, symposia, monographs and ad hoc scientific publications, patents, standards and theses. Articles of popular nature are not included. It is an exhaustive listing of contributions by Indian scientists and technologists in Indian periodicals and those coming in foreign journals.

Biological Abstracts, Philadelphia, The Engineering Index, New York, Excerpta Medica, Amsterdam, Historical Abstracts, Santa Barbara, California, Human Resources Abstracts, California etc. are some other leading abstracting Journals.

ADVANCES, PROGRESS REPORTS, ANNUAL REVIEWS

These types of reports are different from periodical publications. These are critical summary by specialists concerning the development in a particular field. Hence they are very helpful for those who are tracing the developments in different subjects. Advances in Computers, Progress in Aerospace, Annual Review of Information Science and Technology, Annual Review of Anthropology, Annual Review of Sociology, Report on the Progress of Applied Chemistry, Advances in Agronomy etc are some typical publications of this sort.

BIBLIOGRAPHY

Bibliography is considered as the technique of systematically producing descriptive lists of written or published records especially books and similar materials and a list thus compiled is also called bibliography. It is a complete and uncritical list and does not contain any comments. But due to economic factors and human limitations such lists are not exhaustive. Lists given at the end of documents are not bibliography although authors often name it as bibliography. The term bibliography was first used by Louis Jacob de Saint Charles in his "Bibliographia Parisiana" that was published in 1650. Louis Shores, an American Library Scientist, defined bibliography as a "List of written, printed or otherwise produced record of civilization, which may include books, serials, pictures, films, maps, records, manuscripts and any media of communication." According to Dr. S R Ranganathan bibliography is a "list of documents together for some purpose. The purpose is to bring to the attention of the reader an exhaustive or selective list of documents relevant to his pursuit of study or enquiry."

Aims and Objectives

The UNESCO has stated the following aims and functions of bibliography.

1. To enable intellectual workers to learn of publications recording the developments in their fields of interest not only in their own country but also through the world.
2. Promote the effectiveness of a particular project in research.
3. Contribute to the cultural development and enjoyment which are derived from records of learning and culture.
4. Assist in promoting useful applications of existing knowledge and in making the applications which have been developed in one country, widely known to all countries.

The bibliographic apparatus gives access to information. A reader can know very well about the existence of document in a particular field. It saves a lot of effort and time of the reader.

There are three branches of bibliography namely, Systematic or Enumerative Bibliography, Analytical or Critical Bibliography and Historical Bibliography.

Systematic bibliography is the bibliography in its most common usage. In a systematic bibliography the individual books are examined for its subject content and are arranged into a logical and useful manner. Here only minimum essential details about a book are given. Readers can identify the documents in a subject area with the help of this bibliography. As it only enlists the documents they are also known as enumerative bibliography. The items are included according to the discretion of the compiler of the bibliography. Systematic bibliography is basic to other areas of bibliography as it is the prerequisite for identifying an item provided in it.

Types

Some of the various types of bibliographies are as follows:

1. Incunabula : Incunabula is a bibliography that lists the early printed material up to the 15th century. These materials were published in the beginning stage of printing with movable types and these do not adhere to strict rules in arranging parts of a book. "An Index to the early printed books in the British Museum from the Invention of Printing to the Year 1500, with notes from those in the Bodleian Libray" by Robert Proctor published in 2 volumes in 1898-99 and "Konrad Burger's Index", London (1960) are typical titles in this category.

2. Universal Bibliography : This includes all published records not necessarily limited by time, territory, language, subject or form. Compilation of such an extensive bibliography is impractical for compilation. A national Bibliography is perhaps a nearest approach to a universal bibliography. Computerization can perhaps aid in compilation of universal bibliographies.

3. National Bibliography : It includes all documents within a country published and unpublished irrespective of the agency issuing them, covering trade and non-trade items, irrespective of the form, language, subject or time. This may be all books published in a country or on a country or by the citizens of a country or all books published on all citizens of the country and any combination of the above categories. National bibliographies are usually published by Governments or Government Agencies and it is a national heritage. Its purpose is intellectual and is very useful for researchers. The British National Bibliography (London, British Library) and Indian National Bibliography (Calcutta, National Library) are examples o f national bibliographies.

4. Trade Bibliography : This is brought out by large publishing firms or commercial organizations engaged in book trade. They include all kinds of books available for sale by them. These bibliographies are ubiquitous and numerous. Indian Books in Print and Whitaker's Books in Print are typical examples in this category. Trade bibliographies are published with commercial motive.

5. Subject Bibliographies : A subject bibliography is concerned with the listing of all books and other documents on a subject irrespective of time, place or form. It is generally specific in coverage and aims at research workers and others interested in a specialized field. A subject bibliography may be retrospective, current, inclusive of all forms from monographs to government publications.

Author Bibliography

An author bibliography records books articles, monographs etc. written by an author or attributed to him and also includes materials written about the author by others.

Bibliography of Bibliographies or Bibliographic Index

This is a listing of bibliographies recorded in a systematic order by subject, place or by individual. It includes all types of bibliographies in various fields. These help readers to select useful bibliographies. "A World Bibliography of Bibliographies and of Bibliographical Catalogues, Calendars, Abstracts, Digests, Indexes and the Like" by Theodore Besterman published by Societas Bibliographica in 1965-67 is a typical example for this.

UNION CATALOGUES

Union catalogue is defined as "a catalogue listing in one sequence the holding or part of the holdings of two or more libraries." According to William Katz "Union catalogue is an inventory common to several libraries that lists some or all of the their publications maintained in one or more orders of arrangement." In short a union catalogue informs the reader in which library a particular document is available. It can be named as a catalogue of catalogues. Its importance lies in promoting inter library cooperation on local, regional and international level. It is of immense help to one who searches a document from any part of the world.

Uses of Union Catalogues

1. It serves as a tool to locate the availability of books and other documents in different libraries.
2. Once the availability of a document is ascertained it helps readers to borrow a book.
3. It helps in providing reprographic services to readers in any part of the world.
4. Coordination of selection and acquisition programmes of different libraries is facilitated. Thus procurement of costly books can be limited to one or more libraries.
5. It gives an idea of the library resources available within a geographical unit.
6. It is very useful for reference librarians in rendering service to their clientele by guiding the readers as to where a particular item is available.

Types of Union Catalogues

The first type is the local level union catalogue. A union catalogue of documents in the public libraries of Kannur district is an example for this.

The second type is the regional level. It may include the documents available in a region like Malabar, Kerala or South India. For example a union catalogue of books and other documents of the university libraries in Kerala would be would be a regional level union catalogue. The third type is the national level union catalogues. This would be specially helpful for researchers and teachers and the academic community in general to find the availability of a document at the national level.

The fourth type is the international level. This is only in conceptual level and no such catalogues have been published so far.

Form of Material

Depending upon the form of documents included in the union catalogue, there would be a union catalogue of books, periodicals, newspapers, audiovisual materials etc.

The National Union Catalogue of US Library of Congress

The Library of Congress began its union catalogue project in 1901 in an attempt to locate and note the location of a copy of every important book in the United Sates. The work was in card form. With financial assistance from John D. Rockfeller Jr. the collection grew to over 11 million cards. Copies of these cards were distributed to a number of libraries around the country. By 1926 it had more than two million cards arranged in the Library of Congress. It was very unwieldy and therefore since 1940 it was printed. In an effort to simplify research, it was decided in the 1960s to collect and publish all of the references to pre-1956 imprints in a single alphabetical listing. cumulated quarterly, annually, and multi-annually.

Mansell Information/Publishing Ltd. undertook the publishing work. Subsequently it included resources of other libraries also. It also includes specialty catalogues such as the National Union Catalog of Manuscript Collections (NUCMC).

The authority of the US Library of Congress is well established. Therefore the information contained in the National Union Catalogue(NUC) is very reliable. The NUC covers not only the holdings of the Library of Congress but also those of more than 1500 other American and Canadian libraries. It lists all kinds of documents such as books, periodicals, magazines, serials, maps, microforms and music. The pre 1956 imprints is a cumulative NUC up to 1956 and has more than 11 million entries. having 754 volumes, containing over 528,000 pages. It is international in coverage as it includes documents published in different parts of the world and that are available in USA and Canada. The NUC is arranged alphabetically by author and by title where there is no author. It is never both author and title and no subject approach is provided. Now the Library of Congress Union Catalogue is available online.

Union List of Serials in Libraries of the United States and Canada (HW Wilson),British Union Catalogue of Periodicals Butterworth), World List of Scientific Periodicals (Butterworth), A Short -title Catalogue of Books Printed in England by A W Pollard and G R Redgrave London, Bibliographical Society), Union Catalogue of Learned Periodical Publications in South Asia compiled by S R Ranganathan (Indian Library Association), National Union Catalogue of Scientific Serials (NISCAIR, New. Delhi) etc. are some other important union catalogues.

CURRENT INFORMATION SOURCES

Current information sources are very important in keeping abreast with the daily developments in the world of knowledge. News papers are the most popular among these. The morning newspaper briefs us about the day to day events. Weekly publications and popular magazines also give lot of information to its readers. Radio, Television and the Internet are also quick carriers of knowledge to people at large. They have special effects in providing with a vivid picture of the incidents. The presentation of space missions, Independence Day or Republic day celebrations that we watch in the television etc. are very educative for people of all walks of life and leaves vivid impressions about it.

Let us examine some current information sources.

Asian Recorder/Asian News Digest

Asian recorder is a weekly digest of Asian events with index. It provides weekly news summary of current events happening in all countries of Asia as well as those about Asia happening outside the Asian continent.

Here events in all countries of Asia are listed under each country arranged alphabetically. Thus there are 43 country headings. Within each country data is further arranged alphabetically under subjects such as agriculture, commerce and trade, wars, civil wars terrorism worldwide, insurgencies, tribal, ethnic, sectarian conflicts, major world events, global economy and disasters both natural and man-made, including climate change. It consists of three parts.

1. Events in all countries of Asia listed under each country. Thus there are 443 country heads. Within each country data are arranged alphabetically.
2. There are separate sections on international organizations, books, documents, sports, personalities etc. Events about Asia happening in other continents are listed under a separate heading "Asia outside Asia."
3. Two write-ups giving detailed analysis of major events.

This was known as Asian Recorder from 1955-1999, but

on January 1, 2000, its title was changed to Asian News Digest. This is now available in print as well as online. Events, news and news analysis are covered on a day-by-basis in a weekly format both in print and on-line.

The journal provides a million word annual data in 52 weekly issues and also an annual volume compiling all the 52 issues with an annual index compiled country-wise and subject-wise in the alphabetical order to facilitate instant access to the user.

Keesing's World News

Keesing's Record of World Events is published from London since 1931 by Longman. Previously it was known as Keesing's Contemporary Archives. This is a monthly news digest of important world events. It covers all important national and international events without any political or regional bias. Regional experts sift and distill data and news from press reports,, government agencies and other institutions, radio and televisions broadcastings and write concise, comprehensive reports on the critical developments in every country in the world. The main focus of the paper is Europe and the Commonwealth Countries. The news items are also indexed by a full team of experts. References to sources are mentioned. Full texts of important speeches and documents are a special attraction. The arrangement is by country with broad subject headings. Detailed subject reports in certain areas are frequently included. Ephemeral events on sports, arts and films etc. are treated only briefly. This is an excellent tool on international affairs and an invaluable source for researchers.

Keesing's World News Archive (www.keesings.com) was launched in 2007 at the International Studies Association annual meeting in Chicago. Their work constitutes a 76-year archive, totaling nearly 100,000 contemporaneously-written articles, each linked to earlier and related coverage. Its editors select the most historically significant political, social, and economic events, extract critical information from worldwide news sources, and write concise reports. These reports are available in the archive, stripping bias away and correcting errors in the original press reports. Thousands of academic, government, and policy bodies rely on Keesing's for comprehensive, impartial information and news, and the journal is a mainstay of the top libraries and research institutions worldwide.. Today, Keesing's produces 150 articles per month on average.

Search is facilitated by entering multiple terms in the search box combining them with Boolean logic. Search results can be sorted by date (ascending or descending) or by relevance. It's when you look at the full text of an article that Web 2.0 elements surface. At the bottom of the article, you will find a space where you can add your personal tags to the article and write notes. In the collaborative spirit of Web 2.0, you can share your tags and notes with other searchers. You can also search within the article, which is useful since search terms are not highlighted. You can create your own private portfolios. Unlike more static information sources, Keesing's gives you the opportunity to complain about what you see on a page. If you choose to "Report a problem, you get an automated response promising a human follow-up. The power of user-generated tagging for historical events has exciting possibilities. Because Keesing's World News Archive is so new, tags are few and far between. It will be interesting to watch the evolution of the tagging function. Keesing's says it intends to add more of its own tags. Searching the archives is not the only option at the home page. A Breaking History option appears directly under Search the Archive. This provides timelines on predefined topics, such as bird flu. According to publisher, Jonathan Hixon, "This venture marks our entry into the world of collaboration with developers, researchers, historians, and, hopefully, other publishers. We developed our software on an open source content management system developed in Australia, which is now being looked at by other publishers and could well lead to more compatible and consistent platforms for data."

REFERENCES

Dhiman, Anil K and Yashoda Rani: Learn information and reference sources and services.New Delhi, ESS ESS, 2005.

Gates, JK: Guide to the use of libraries and information sources.New York, McGraw-Hill, 1979.

Grogan, Denis: Science and technology: An introduction to the literature. London,Bingly, 1982.

Katz, William A: Introduction to reference work. New York, McGraw Hill, 1982.

Krishan Kumar: Reference service. New Delhi, Vikas, 2008

Kumar, PSG: Information sources and services: Theory and practices.New Delhi, BR Publishing Corporation, 2004.

Ranganathan,SR: Reference service and bibliography. Madras, Madras Library Association, 1940

Shores, William: Basic reference sources. Chicago, ALA, 1954

Winchel, CM: Guide to reference books. Chicago, ALA

Chapter

5

Reference Service

Reference service is the process of establishing contact between a reader and his documents in a personal way. The reader wants the documents that will serve his requirements, but he may not be aware of its availability. Dr. Ranganathan describes this as the contact between the right reader and the right book at the right time and in the right personal way." Here Ranganathan emphasizes on personal service to each user. Margaret Hutchins says "Reference work includes the direct, personal aid within a library to persons in search of information for whatever purpose, and also various library activities especially aimed at making information as easily available as possible." The librarian has to take special interest in getting the document that a reader requires. This is a personal service. The librarian can depend on the document available in his library or can resort to document in other libraries or get the help of other persons. Reference service is of two types. Ready reference service and long range reference.

READY REFERENCE SERVICE

Ready reference service, as the term connotes is providing answers for simple queries of the readers without too much time and effort. According to Dr. Ranganathan "Ready reference service is reference service finished in a very short time in a moment if possible" A typical question may be who the first president of the Indian Union was or who invented the steam engine etc. Thus the concept of ready reference service is based on duration of time. Ready reference service is like a fact finding service. Sometimes the reference queries made by the readers may be very simple and the answers can be given immediately by the librarian by referring an encyclopedia or yearbook and sometimes even without referring to any documents at all. The librarian can also help the reader by providing a document that would easily help him to find the answer for himself. In some cases the librarian has to make detailed discussion with the readers in order to get an idea of the right information he requires.

To the question of why reference service has to be provided to a reader, Dr. Ranganathan states that a reference book may differ from an ordinary book in the arrangement, subject, area and period of coverage. Therefore he needs help from the librarian in finding out information from them. Sometimes the ordinary reader may take too much time to extract information but a librarian will be able to help him out very easily. On the manner of ready reference service he says that there are three interrelated processes in it. They are preparation, service and assimilation. Preparation is the process taking place behind the curtain. He should anticipate the needs of the readers and procure books and other reference materials in advance. He should procure reference books and browse through it to get a bird's eye view of its contents. The new editions should be substituted with the older ones. A file consisting of ephemeral materials like

Newspaper cuttings magazines etc. should be maintained

Only the right kind of attitude and preparation can enable a librarian to render effective service. Service involves directing the inquirer along the right paths so that he can find the information for himself, providing the information directly to the user and it also implies imparting training to the user community in the efficient use of the library. It helps to learn more from our experience. Assimilation or absorption of information on the part of the librarian will be helpful in improving library tools and services.

The nature of reference service will vary from library to library. In the case of a special library the questions raised by the reader would be very specific and the librarian should preferably maintain special files consisting of newspaper clippings, pamphlets, prospectus of different courses of study, circulars, news bulletins etc. In his daily work he should try to assimilate important information he may come across keeping in mind the potential users he is likely to come across in future. A reference librarian should also be aware of the activities of other departments in the library, especially the acquisition and cataloguing departments whereby he would become more familiar with the collection of the library. In academic and special libraries the library should conduct regular orientation programmes to train the members in the use of the resources of the library. Certain members of the library may belong to the VIP category. They would deserve special treatment and the information may have to be delivered at their office personally.

LONG RANGE REFERENCE SERVICE

Long range reference service has been necessitated by the advanced outlook in the provision of library service. The requirements of members in a special or academic library demands provision of long range reference service. However it is not totally absent in other libraries. As the term indicates, long range reference service involves more time and effort from the part of the librarian to get the information.

There is no specific limit on the time required. Dr. Ranganathan says "Few long range reference questions take less than half an hour, while some take a whole day and even weeks." In contrast to ready reference service that can be very often provided with the help of a ready reference tool, long range reference service requires the perusal of journal articles, books, non-book materials etc. Sometimes the search has to be extended to other libraries or institutions of learning. The librarian should be well aware of the world of learning for the effective rendering of long range reference service. Some times the information sought may be very specific like allergic diseases caused by pollen of trees of foreign origin or Impact of western culture in India. Answers to such questions would require the perusal of a number of information sources and even unpublished materials. Sometimes the relevant information may be in a foreign language demanding translation service. Multiple forms of information sources like microfilms, CD-ROMs and other audiovisual media are also to be procured by the librarian. The fifth law of library science as enunciated by Dr. Ranganathan, "Save the time of the reader", holds the librarian duty bound to provide long range reference service to every reader to the maximum possible extent.

Dr. Ranganathan, on the question of what constitutes long range reference service says that the time involved in finding out information differentiates long range from the ready reference service. He says that long range reference service starts with ready reference sources but continues to more sophisticated information sources and to other libraries and even individuals. Thus it would be a prolonged search.

The information sought may be highly specialized and from a particular view point. Information available in foreign languages necessitates translation. Very recent information may not be available in reference books and newspapers and magazines have to be referred for finding the correct information. On the question of why long range reference service has become very complicated, Dr. Ranganathan says that increase in literature has become so numerous especially in the field of science and technology that the librarian has to work hard to cater to the requirements of the readers. In this context Ranganathan compares the search for information as searching for a needle in a haystack. Users would appreciate reference service very much if it can lead to saving of time. By saving the time of readers from the intellectual and administrative elitist classes, the librarian is contributing to the betterment and material advancement of the society. An experienced and committed reference librarian can elicit high respect and the library profession will get more recognition from the society.

In the modern era the need for long range reference service is all the more demanding. Research scholars, scientists, business executives, journalists, politicians and numerous other professionals are depending more and more on libraries for their information needs. The librarians should be well groomed to meet their demands and equipped with all relevant materials to meet the exigencies of enquiries from their clientele.

According to Dr.Ranganathan, long range reference service involves, preparation, service and assimilation. These are three interrelated processes. The preparation involves activities such as i)Acquiring knowledge of the subject ii)Scanning of information sources iii)Gathering of information; and iv) Recording of information. In the phase of service the activities such as Enunciation of the requirements of the users, search of documents or information and supply of information or documents are carried out. While in the assimilation phase the reference librarian shares his experiences with his colleagues in the reference section.

Ready reference and long range reference services differ with respect to time, source of information and nature of information sought. Ready reference service is limited to ready reference sources and we are mainly concerned with facts. Long range reference service would take half an hour to days or even weeks. The information gathered can be used in answering future queries in which case it transforms into a ready reference service. Long range service is going to be prominent as knowledge advances and readers increase. The capacity of a librarian to answer to reference queries enhances his personality and acceptance in the society.

As a first step to this a librarian should try to acquire a fairly good awareness in the subject areas in which the members are interested. His knowledge is that of a literature specialist and not a subject specialist. A users' survey can identify the subject fields in which the readers are interested. The emphasis on collection build up is related to the nature of the clientele, type of library, and the objectives of the library. He should be in a position to scan the published materials. A librarian should develop a vision to include books of current interest and also anticipate potential demand from the part of the readers. He should always be in the look out for the latest announcements on new documents that are published. The latest editions of reference sources should be procured. Personal contact with the readers especially the scholars and sister institutions will provide him with a better awareness with the forthcoming publications. The acquired materials should be processed and made ready for immediate use. Outdated books and other materials should be weeded out so that the readers are not misled and the pressure on library space is avoided.

REFERENCES

Documentation Research and Training Centre(Bangalore): Seminar on Reference Service: Working papers and Proceedings, Bangalore, DRTC, 1971.

Krishan Kumar: Reference Service. New Delhi, Vikas, 2008.

Ranganathan, SR: Reference Service. Bombay, Asia Pub.House, 1961.

Chapter

6

User Education

Educating a user is very essential for the successful functioning of any system which is new or complex. Today a modern library is such a system which demands suitable user education for its users. According to T.D Wilson ' user education is the process whereby potential users of information or those concerned with the creation of national information policies, are made aware of the value of information in specialised fields of activity and in everyday life, are instilled to use with positive attitudes towards the need to seek information, and are motivated to use or develop information resources'. Mews defines 'user education is that topic as instruction given to readers to help them make the best use of a library'. Freeman and Maltby state that 'User education can be seen as a major strand within a 'study skills' programme equipping the trainees with the knowledge and abilities to use libraries and information effectively and confidently; a skill of inestimable and enduring value to any manager or administrator who has to handle and evaluate the flow of information emanating from official or non official sources'. Wajid Ahmad Alivi defines user education 'as that facet of library service, which is concerned with educating the library users in efficient use of library resources so that they are able to exploit them to the best of their advantage'.

UNESCO states user education as any effort or programme, which will guide and instruct existing and potential users, individually or collectively with objective of facilitating:

i) the recognition of their own information needs;

ii) the formalisation of their needs;

iii) the effective and efficient use of information service; as well as

iv) the assessment of these services.

To quote Rabindra Nath Tagore 'The reality is not that the readers create library but the fact is that the library makes the readers' It is felt that readers and library are the supplement of each one. Therefore all efforts should be made which are responsible for familiarising reader to the library or fully helpful in getting use of the library. One of the efforts in this direction is imparting user education in libraries.

User education in the present IT environment needs a wide connotation. Hence user education in the present scenario can be defined as a fostering programme whereby the users of information are equipped with awareness of formalisation of their needs, knowledge and experience of general as well as specific information sources, basic research and study, library and information skills to identify, find, evaluate and select the best information for life-long perpetual education. The analysis of the above definitions bring out the fact that any instruction or programme of information provided by libraries to users, to enable them to make more efficient and independent use of library resources and services.

WHY USER EDUCATION?

Why should user education be conducted in libraries? It is based on the assumption that to know how to use a library is an essential part of the education to prepare the academic community for the continuous process of self education once the formal education is completed. Cuming opined that 'to learn how to use a library and to acquire interested love of reading are important elements of education'. There are a number of educational and library environments which necessitate user education as an important service for the effective utilisation of the library resources. They are discussed below.

i) Quantitative Growth of Information

Information is generated through a number of channels such as printed media and mass media. With regard to printed media 20th century witnessed an exponential growth. It is estimated that literature doubles within a range of 5-10 years in Science and Technology and 7-13 years in Social Science subjects. It is interesting to note that the growth of literature is roughly three times faster than the global population. Because of the incessant growth of information, today we are living in an age of information explosion or information deluge. This phenomenon created a lot of problems to information seekers for information retrieval exhaustively and expeditiously with precision. Besides, 'information pollution' is another problem faced by the user community. Thus the users will be in a state of drowning in information but starving for knowledge, unless the information managers try to provide user education on information use.

ii) Growth in the number of Inter disciplinary and Multidisciplinary Courses

A number of inter disciplinary and multidisciplinary courses and research are being conducted by various academic institutions. These new courses and multi disciplinary research bring great problems to users in the location and retrieval of information for study and research. This demands proper instruction to these categories of users in the search process and search strategy for collecting information from various sources from a variety of subjects.

iii) Artificiality in the Library System

A modern library is becoming more and more artificial day by day to the users. The artificiality is usually seen in the physical forms of catalogues, kinds of catalogue entries, notation in classification, organisation of information in the primary, secondary, tertiary sources, sophisticated information services including computer-based information retrieval, on-line information retrieval, web enabled services etc. which create an atmosphere of unfamiliarity for the users. This unfamiliarity leads to under utilisation of library resources and services. For the effective utilisation of resources and services appropriate user education programmes are necessary.

v) Revolutionary changes in the Physical forms of Documents.

The revolutionary changes in the physical forms of documents create problems to information users. Today, libraries acquire a good number of information sources in the digital form such as magnetic tape, CD-ROMs, DVDs etc. In fact we are going at a faster rate towards the paperless age as envisaged by Lancaster. The effective use of digital sources demands proper user instruction among users.

vi) Limited Fiscal Resources

It is said that no library can claim to be the richest in resources. Due to the limited financial allocation each library is not having adequate staff therefore readers are not properly given personal assistance. They assist to the readers for accessing the reading materials and this necessitate user education.

vii) The emphasis on Self Study

The library is also the centre of independent study. This role was well accepted when concepts like 'Teaching Library' and 'Library College' were developed in the western countries. The Montieth college experiment, Michigan, USA and Earlham college experiment, Indiana, USA which attracted the distant learners proved the validity of the above concepts. Fjallbrant and Malley observe that 'recent trends in education have increased the need for helping the library user. The emphasis on self education has led to the increased use of tutorials, seminars, projects and guided reading as teaching methods and less reliance on formal lessons and lectures. There is an implicit assumption that the learner is capable of finding material relevant to his needs'.

The concept of 'Teaching Library' has been recognised in the report of the library committee of the Swarthmore College. In this report Williamson pointed out the following features of the teaching library as i) that experience and proficiency in the use of library materials be made an integral part of courses of instruction ii) that the curriculum assures the experience in self instruction through independent learning ; and c) that each student be required to demonstrate some skills at independent inquiry by spending at least one semester for independent study.

The concept of 'Library college' is another revolutionary idea developed in the western field. The concept is that class room teaching is totally dispensed with and the library takes its place. According to Blake as the library college is based on the concept of independent study each individual student learning primarily by reading - the college needs to be bibliographically sophisticated and one of its main functions should be to guide the students into the resources of the library. For the maximum exploitation of information by users, librarians should play the role of teacher-librarians by providing appropriate user education programmes to library users.

GOALS AND OBJECTIVES OF USER EDUCATION

In considering the goals and objectives for library user education, one becomes aware that, if expressed at all, these tend to be very vague. Thus Lubans stated that ' several locally developed guidelines for instruction in library skills have been drawn up but these guidelines are rarely based on basic objectives. Similarly, Stevenson has made the statement that ' few libraries have expressed either the aims or objectives for reader instruction'. The goals and objectives for programmes of library user education must be in agreement with the aims and goals of the parent institution to which the library is attached. According to Allen and others the goals and objectives of user education are: i) A general orientation or initiation for the users to available facilities and resources; ii) the teaching of basic research skills and strategies; and iii) instruction regarding the organisation of the literature and reference tools in various disciplines

FACETS OF USER EDUCATION

User education consists of the following interrelated facets or components.

- User Awareness

- Library Orientation
- Bibliographic Instruction
- Interest Profiling

User Awareness

User awareness is an initial step in user education preceding library orientation. It aims to increase user awareness of the library as a primary source of information and as an agency to which users may turn for assistance with their information needs. It is achieved through publicizing the library, with special reference to its resources and services available to the user community.

Library Orientation

Library orientation aims at acquainting the freshman or new member with some of the basis concerning the library use. It is concerned with introducing the user to the general techniques of library usages and services available in library and in particular, to the organisation, services and layout of particular library. According to Dr. Ranganathan, ' New library members coming first time in the library have difficulties and certain confusions, as a result they can not use the library facilities freely. To help those readers and to explain them that library is an useful institution, given an orientation' It is intended: i) to familiarise users with the physical layout and the procedures for using the library units relevant to their needs; ii) to make users aware of the staff that is available to assist them and to make users comfortable seeking assistance; iii) to inform users about basic library holdings records such as the card catalogue and serials list that can be used to locate material within the system. In fact orientation is concerned with introducing the users to the library so that they become aware of physical location of different sections, staff, collections and services.

Nancy Fjallbrant states that during orientation the new members should be explained the following as the course content of the programme.

i) The characteristics of book and its various parts;

ii) Library functions, services and facilities;

iii) Library ethics including library rules, care of books etc;

iv) General arrangement of the library including provision of open access sections;

v) Variety of collections and their location;

vi) The use of reference books including bibliographies;

vii) The scheme of classification being used;

viii) The conventions which form the basis of the library catalogue;

ix) Taking of notes from documents; and

x) Compilation of bibliographies etc.

The above course programme may be suitably designed to new members of various types of libraries such as public libraries, school libraries, college libraries, university libraries and special libraries depending upon the nature, type and levels of users.

In a public library users are heterogeneous in character. The orientation programme should be taken into consideration the characteristics of public libraries in designing the course programme. The orientation programme should be carried out throughout the year since the admission of the new members in a public library is through out a year. As far as possible orientation should be done on individual basis or in small groups

In school libraries initiation or orientation programme should be integrated into the total educational programme.

It can be related to class room work and laboratory work. Library hour can be utilized for the purpose of orientation. Orientation can be conducted during the beginning of an academic year.

The new comers in colleges and universities can be grouped as: Undergraduate, Graduate, Post-graduate and research levels. The orientation programmes can be arranged in colleges and University libraries during the beginning of the academic year. All these groups should be given orientation in different groups at separate time with appropriate course content..

A special library specialises in a particular subject or group of subjects usually catering to a small groups of users. Due to the very nature, it is possible to provide orientation on individual basis. Orientation may be given in the area of literature in the field of research, services, information available from various information systems at the national and international levels etc.

Bibliographic Instruction

Bibliographic instruction is the process whereby library staff help users to gain access to information, both by formal instructional methods and training on the spot. A variety of techniques will be used, including multimedia and interactive systems. According to Stevenson, bibliographic instruction is 'introduction to the user of the information resources available in particular subject disciplines and the techniques of making use of those resources'. Lewis and Foster state that as ' education in the systematic use of information sources,. Bibliographic instruction is meant to help users take maximum advantage of library resources to meet their information needs. To achieve this goal, bibliographic instruction programme must be designed: i) To improve users' skills in making effective use of library collections, services, and staff ; and ii) to increase users' abilities to make independent use of these resources.

Bibliographic instruction is discipline -specific library instruction. These are presentations tailored to a specific class topic. They can include a very detailed instruction on using discipline specific databases, information on the topic in other databases, a selection of materials on the topic, specific in searching for information on the internet on the topic and others. They can also be tailored to a specific course assignment.

Interest Profiling

Interest profiling is a means to ascertain the information needs of users in a library. This consists of creating profiles of the users, who are to be provided bibliographic instruction. A profile consists of i) Name of the user; ii) Category of users; iii) Department/ Institution; iv) Mailing address; v) Contact numbers; vi) E-mail address; vii) Languages known; viii) Specific topic of research/ Areas of subject interest; ix) Other topics/ Other areas of interest ; x) Favoured author(s);xi) Preferred journal(s) etc. Gathering of information for a profile is an important step. A Proforma or profile card is designed with the information given above. Each user should be requested to fill up the Proforma. The filled up Proforma will act as the base line data for the user education programme.

COURSE PROGRAMME

Stuart Wyne Miller states that a library use instruction programme is 'a procedure whereby students are taught to use library devices such as the card catalogue, bibliographical tools such as periodical indexes, subject reference sources etc and to utilise effective search strategies in the library' Thus a user education or user instruction programme aims to teach the users, library devices, bibliographical tools and utilisation of effective search strategies in a library.

The courses include i) Course related library instruction, which focuses on particular skills and tools that are helpful for a particular assignment; ii) Course integrated library instruction which is an integrated library instruction refers to library instruction that is incorporated into the regular academic programme; iii) Formal course in bibliography. In this course users may be instructed in the use of the library by means of a formal course in bibliography.

METHODS AND MEDIA OF USER EDUCATION

A number of methods are available for imparting user education programmes in libraries. A single method may not be suitable for effective instruction. Hence a combination of methods may be adopted based on the type of user population and the objectivity of the course content.

The methods of user education can be categorised into direct methods and indirect methods. The direct methods are:

- Orientation lectures/courses
- Conducted library tour
- Reader librarian dialogue while rendering reference service or when reader is browsing the library catalogue
- Librarian's participation in the Reader's writing
- At informal meetings at educational or cultural functions.

The Indirect methods include

- Library Guides
- Display
- Circulation of documentation lists
- Technological gatekeepers
- Audio-visual aids.

Nancy Fjallbrant has given the following classification for group instruction, individual instruction and both group and individual instruction.

For group instruction methods like lecture method, seminar method and guided tour are included. While for individual instruction methods such as practical exercise, self instructional materials individual help etc are included. In the case of both group and individual instruction methods such as films, video tape, tape slide, audio tape and printed media such as books, printed guides etc are used.

PROGRAMMED INSTRUCTION

Programmed instruction is a course of instruction in which the subject matter to be instructed is divided into logical sequence of short items. The steps involved in learning each item allows a user to check immediately the correctness or suitability of his response. Programmed instruction can be carried out through a work book, handbook, Library Path Finder, audio-visual programmes or computer aided learning or computer aided instruction.

Computer -Assisted Learning(CAL) or computer-assisted Instruction (CAI) is a useful means of programmed instruction for teaching in the use of more complex bibliographic tools. Whereas point-of-use instruction is generally limited to a basic explanation of a tool, with CAI the computer may be used to demonstrate solutions to problems, to test the user's comprehension of the explanation, and provide feedback to the students on the correctness of their answers, thus reinforcing learning. Possible topics for the utilisation of CAI in the general libraries include the card catalogue and certain indexes which are especially difficult to use. To-day a number of user-friendly softwares are available, which provide guidance to the user at his level, taking him step by step in a friendly manner.

EVALUATION

Systematic evaluation of the process of user education programmes should be an essential aspect of user education. Immediate effects of user education programmes have been measured successfully but techniques for measuring its long term effect have not been developed fully. The methods used for the evaluation of user education programmes include: i)Comparative evaluation; ii)Normative evaluation; and iii) Illuminative or responsive evaluation.

Comparative evaluation is also known as psychometric evaluation. A group of users or target population is tested before the course and then submitted to different instructional methods. The users are again post tested. For testing, psychometric tests consisting of achievement tests or attitude scales are made use of. While in the normative evaluation, evaluation of the programme is done on the basis of prescribed normative criteria. It may take the form of objectives. This is based on how far the programme achieved in fulfilling the formulated objectives. Illuminative evaluation is a rich and creative development. Parlett and Hamilton state the aims of illuminative evaluation are to 'study the innovatory project; how it operates; how it is influenced by the various school situations in which it is applied; what those directly concerned regard as its advantages and disadvantages ; and how students' intellectual tasks and academic experiences are most affected. It aims to discover and document what it is like to be participating in the scheme, whether as teacher or pupil; and in addition, to discern ad discuss the innovation's most significant features, recurring concomitants, and critical process. In short it seeks to address and to illuminate a complex array of questions.'

REFERENCES

Fjallbrant, Nancy and Stevenson,Malcolm: User education in libraries.London, Clive Bingly, 1978.

Fleming, Hugh, Ed: User education in academic libraries.London,LA, 1990

Guskin, Allen E, et al: The academic library as a teaching library : a role for the 1980s. Library Trends, 1979.

Hamilton, D and Parlett, M: Evaluatin as illumination. In D Tawney,ed. Curriculum evaluation today: trends and implications. London, Macmillan, 1976.

Hills, R J, Ed: Information package on teaching methods for librarians. London, The British Library, 1979.

Kirk, Thomas G: Bibliographic instruction - a review of research'. In conference on the Evaluation of library instruction, Denver(1973). Evaluating library instruction. ed.by Richar B Beeler, Michigan, Pierian Press, 1975.

Krishan Kumar: Reference service.5thed. Bangalore, Vikas Pub.House,1982.

Lewis, David and Foster, Allan: Tuition in library and literature use.In George Jefferson and GCK Smith-Bunett. The college library. London,Clive Bingly, 1978

Lubans, John: Educating the library use. New York, R R Bowker,1974.

Miller, Stuart Wayne: Library use instruction in selected American colleges.Illinois, University of Illinois Graduate school of Library Science,1978.

Ranganathan, SR: Reference Service.ed.2.Bombay, Asia Pub.1961

Sehal, RL: User education in computer based libraries.New Delhi, ESS ESS1998.

Stevenson, M B: User education programmes. Boston.Spa. The British Library, 1977.

Wilson, TD: Guidelines for developing and implementing a national plan for training in information use., 1980.

Chapter

7

User Studies

In an information system user is an important component. But this aspect was neglected by the librarians and information managers for a long time. Access to relevant information is highly essential particularly in industrial, research and development sectors. Right information to the right user can pave way to new directions to research and development. It is imperative that to achieve this objective we should understand the library user, how they interact with the system, their pattern of search and their pertinent information requirements.

USERS

In a library or an information centre the users are the last link or the recipients of information in the communication cycle. There are a number of terms used as synonyms or near synonyms to user as patron, client, member and customer. Of these, user is the preferred term. According to Whittaker a user may be defined as a person who uses one or more library services at least once a year.

Users are individuals who can be divided into different categories on the basis of tasks assigned to them in a library organisation.

The users of one type of library are different from those of another library. In a public library the users are mainly children, students, housewives, farmers, retired persons, neo-literates and even researchers. In an academic library the users are students, teachers and researchers whereas in a special library the users are mainly researchers or specialists or special group of users for whom the library is intended. From what is stated above, it can be assumed that in the public libraries the users are heterogeneous and in the academic and special libraries the users are almost homogeneous in nature. For an effective information service an information manager should ascertain the information requirements of his library users.

According to Kunz information users can be categorised mainly into four groups on the basis of their approach to information in libraries. They are:

i) *Potential user* - the one who needs information which can be provided by specific services;

ii) *The expected user* - the one who is known to have the intention of using certain information services;

iii) *The actual user* - the one who derives a measurable advantages from it or not; and

iv) *The beneficiary user* - the one who derives a measurable advantage from information services.

User groups may be categorised into a number of ways. They can be divided into internal users and external users. According to Whittaker user community is classified on the basis of services they availed by them and are the following.

i) *General readers* : This type of user groups, say for

example, associated with public libraries generally use light reading materials;

ii) *Subject reader* : This type of users concentrate their use of library materials on a subject field, the field they are working or specialising;

iii) *Special readers* : The users placed in this group are those with special needs, because of disabilities either physical or mental ; and

iv) *Non-reading users* : Non-reading users are made up of sub-groups who make use of library materials, but not reading materials. A user coming into the library just to borrow a video is an example of non-reading user.

Another classification of users is: personal users, surrogate users and corporate users. Personal users are those who avails library services for their own individual needs. A user who uses a library service on behalf of someone else is known as surrogate user. The corporate user is also one who uses the library's services on behalf of another, that is the organisation that sends him to the library. Dr. S.R. Ranganathan has grouped user community on the basis of various types of reference services enunciated by him. They are: The freshman, ordinary inquirer, specialist inquirer and general reader. Here the freshman is the new member of a library, ordinary inquirer is ordinary reader, specialist inquirer is one who specialise in a narrow field or specialist whereas general readers are the assorted group of users which are not included in any of the above groups. In order to satisfy these four types of users, Ranganathan has conceived four types of services such as initiation or orientation, ready reference service, long range reference service and general help to general readers respectively.

There are certain people who because of their lifestyles or other environmental problems can't become members of libraries in their vicinity and make use of the library resources. They are non-users. It is the duty of the librarian especially in public libraries to convert non-users or 'on lookers' into potential and habitual users of such libraries. There are a number of ways by which a librarian can attract such users into libraries by means of extension activities or other publicity methods. The duty of librarian is more important to convert non-users into habitual users and mould them as capable citizens just like other citizens who are engaged in social development.

INFORMATION NEEDS AND USERS

The main objective of a library or information system is to satisfy the information needs of users. Information needs refer to individual needs of users regarding information which should be satisfied by the specific information needed by him. There are two types of needs. One relates to the kind of message, in terms of subject, currency etc and the other relates to means of supplying them. Information needs of a user depend on a number of factors such as work activity, discipline and availability of facilities. They can be primarily divided into two types viz current awareness and adhoc need. In the current awareness mode the users require current information in their field of specialisation or interest whereas in the adhoc type it is needed to satisfy a specific purpose. Oats opines that two types of information needs exist in any organisation. They are information about organisation itself and information about external environment in which the organisation is to function.

There are a number of factors that affect information needs of users. Paisley observed that the following factors influence the information needs of user community.

i) The range of information sources available;

ii) The use in which the information be put;

iii) The background, motivation, professional orientation and other individual characteristics of the users;

iv) The social, political and economic system surrounding the use; and

v) The consequences of information use.

Information need is a multifaceted concept which is generally dynamic in users. Guha has stated that there are four types of information needs or approaches recognised by users. They are : Current approach; Everyday approach; Exhaustive approach; and Brushing up approach. The current approach is that which users require to keep abreast of the nascent developments in his field of specialisation/interest. Everyday approach is sought for specific piece of information required by the user during the day to day investigation of facts or data. The exhaustive approach is sought when a researcher wants to have a comprehensive detail about a specific topic on the field of study. Catching up approach is adopted in situations where a particular user requires information pertaining to related subjects fields.

Lohmann mentions 8 user characteristics that, if evaluated, would help the librarian in his efforts to satisfy user needs. These are functional reading level, visual level, personality level, capacity level, satisfaction level, interest level, variability level and vocational-avocational level. Systematic study of user community will reveal the varied characteristics of users seeking information. This will give necessary basic guidelines to librarians to serve various types of user groups.

USER STUDIES

The concept of user studies has been defined variously by different schools of thought. According to Wysoki, user studies or use studies could be concerned with understanding information processing activities of the users. Britain defined user studies as, empirical studies of the use of, demand or need for, information are usually called user studies. The working definition of user study adopted by Centre for Research on user studies is that 'the general objectives of research on users is to further understanding of the processes of information transfer. This may be lead to the improvement of information transfer systems of all types and to have implications for the organisation of communication, the distribution of researcher and the relationships between systems'. In the light of the above definition a study which is focussed on users to understand directly or indirectly their information needs, use behaviour and use pattern is usually called user study.

An early user study in the field was conducted in the late 1930s by Louis R Wilson. The study was an attempt to investigate the distribution and status of libraries in the United States. When we trace the development of user studies it will be seen that it was activated by two international conferences viz Royal Societies' conference in London in 1948 and the Washington conference in 1958. A study entitled ' pilot study on the use of scientific literature by scientists conducted by Ralph R Shaw is considered as another pioneer study in this direction. There was comprehensive bibliography on user studies compiled by Davis and Baily in 1964 containing 438 studies. It is reported by Crawford that by 1977 more than 1000 important studies including state-of -the art reports and review reports were also published. User studies were developed to certain extent because of the tremendous growth in Science and Technology subsequent to world war II.

One of the turning points in the history of user studies was the establishment of the Centre for Research on User Studies(CRUS). The Centre was established by the British

Library Research and Development division at the University of Sheffield towards the end of 1975. The Centre became fully functional on 1st January 1976. The purpose of the Centre is to create a national centre to act as a focus for research in user studies which would improve the utility of user studies by overcoming problems and providing a permanent core of expertise in research methods available to other researchers. The other objectives of the Centre are education and training, advice and consultancy service, information service and publication specifically in the areas of user studies. The establishment of the Centre for Research on user studies is a testimony to the importance of the subject field. This centre can give necessary directions to conduct better and fruitful studies in the field in order to provide user-oriented information services from libraries and information centres in the years to come.

WHY USER STUDIES?

There are a number of objectives for conducting user studies in libraries. They are:

i) To judge the limitations of library system and services;

ii) To identify the levels and kinds of user needs;

iii) To exploit library resources with less money, time and energy;

iv) To enhance the quality of acquisition and collection;

v) To identify the limitations or problems which seem to discourage the use of the library;

vi) To predict future information demands and requirements; and

vii) To design and develop need-based and user-based information system.

CLASSIFICATION OF USER STUDIES

There are a number of classifications available in the various types of user studies. Cronin opines that in the information field, user studies may be either descriptive or prescriptive. A descriptive study describes how information transfer takes place in relation to a particular user population. But a prescriptive study will go one step further and suggest ways by which the prevailing system or product could be modified or upgraded to ensure a greater degree of user satisfaction.

Herbert Menzel has categorised user studies broadly into three. They are behaviour studies, use studies and information flow studies. Studies which are conducted to find out the pattern of overall interaction of the users' community with the communication system, without reference to any specific information receiving event, are called communication behaviour studies. Studies which are conducted to find out the use of any communication medium such as primary periodical, secondary periodical, reference sources etc are called use studies, whereas information flow studies are those that are conducted to find out the flow of information in the communication system. Menzel has also given another classification of user studies in a study entitled 'Information needs and uses in Science and Technology which was published in Annual Review of Information Science and Technology, 1966. In this study he has grouped user studies into channel studies, utility studies, studies of failures and near misses, exposure by phase research, exposure of measures of success, critical incident studies, critical incident decision studies, dissemination studies etc. Dervin and Nilan describe three approaches that are evident in the literature of user studies. They are : i) the user-value approach which focuses on perception of utility and value of information systems; ii) the sense making approach, which examines the way people make sense of their words and how information is used in this process; and iii) the anomalous states of knowledge(ASK) approach which examines how people seek information concerning situation about which their knowledge is incomplete.

TECHNIQUES

A number of techniques that are evolved from Social sciences are available as methods in user studies. Wood has reviewed and classified the methods that have been employed in studies of information users and their needs. He lists the following methods : Questionnaires, Interviews, Diary methods, Observation and Analysis of library data.

Guha has categorised a number of methods under three major heads: General or conventional methods, indirect methods and special and unconventional methods.

GENERAL OR CONVENTIONAL METHODS

General or conventional methods include methods like questionnaire, interview, diary and observation. Of these, questionnaire and interview methods are very popular among investigators engaged in user studies.

A questionnaire is a set of questions framed with a view to ascertain the user needs, use pattern and use behaviour. There are two types of questionnaires : structured and unstructured. A structured questionnaire is generally used for the survey conducted by the questionnaire method. But unstructured questionnaire is used as a tool to conduct structured interview. A questionnaire may contain different types of questions. Questions can be categorised as factual, general, open, closed, mixed etc on the basis of purpose and function, form, nature etc.

In the designing of a questionnaire, due attention should be given by the investigator keeping in view the do's and don't. Consultation with experts should also be attempted in the preparation of a questionnaire. After the preparation of the questionnaire it should be subjected to pre-test by getting the questionnaire filled up by few representative users from the population under study. In the light of pre-test the final form of the questionnaire has to be decided. The questionnaire should be accompanied by a covering letter stating the objective of the study and requesting the whole hearted cooperation of the respondent. The name and address of the investigator should also be given therein. The present trend in user studies shows that the majority of the investigators use the questionnaire method as one of the important techniques for data collection. This may be due to the simplicity of the method and the convenience in conducting a survey study. If the population is large and geographically scattered, questionnaire method is more suitable, less expensive and quick when compared to other methods.

Interview is another popular method which can be used for data collection in user studies. There are two types of interviews: structured and unstructured. Structured interview is conducted by using a pre-designed questionnaire. In the unstructured interview the investigator may not be using a pre-designed questionnaire. There is also no fixed order of questions. In fact, there is only some sort of dialogue between the respondent and the investigator. For a large and geographically dispersed population this method is not suitable. The data collection by this method is expensive and time consuming.

Methods such as diary method and observation methods are other conventional methods. Diary method is that in which users under study are asked to keep a detailed record of particular information activities such as reading, information search, discussion etc. Observation is another important method. There are two types of observations: participant observation and non-participant observation. Individual observation of various information activities is taken for the collection of data. For example a study of catalogue use in a library or study on use of various types of communication media in a library etc this method is more suitable for data collection. This method is time consuming and expensive when compared to questionnaire method.

INDIRECT METHODS

Indirect methods include analysis of library records and citation analysis. On the basis of materials used by the authors, investigators can ascertain the user's information requirements indirectly. For the analysis of library records important records such as circulation statistics, interlibrary loan registers, personal indexes used by the researchers, service demand slips in the reference section, date label slips etc can be used. An analysis of the above records will provide a partial view of user needs or users' information requirements.

Citation analysis is a popular indirect method that can be used as a technique for user study. Citations or references provided by authors in their documents become the basis of citation analysis. The implicit assumption is that the cited documents are used by the authors and this will be the index to the nature of materials required by the users. When compared to other methods, citation analysis is generally treated as unbiased. However, it has a number of demerits such as :

i) Citation analysis will give only a partial idea about the use of materials since, secondary and tertiary sources, non-documentary sources etc the authors are not usually cited although their works are perused ;

ii) The possibility of citing prestigious authors' title, even if these are not really used ;

iii) The possibility of self citation by certain authors etc.

SPECIAL AND UNCONVENTIONAL METHODS

Special and unconventional methods include computer feedback which make use of records obtained as by-products of a computer search. The wider use of computer in libraries can bring this technique into an effective one in ascertaining users' information requirements. By unconventional methods, the investigator tries to know the way in which scientists work and make use of the formal and informal channels of communication by using biographical, autobiographical sources etc.

Each method has its own merits and demerits. Investigators should choose the technique which is very suitable to the population under study. More than one method can be used by the investigator in cases where one method is inadequate in the collection of data.

HOW TO CONDUCT A USER STUDY

It is felt that it would be appropriate to mention here how a user study can be conducted. The practices followed by the investigators may vary from one investigator to another. But as a general approach, the following steps can be used for conducting a user study.

i) Identification of the problem

An investigator should identify the problem to be studied in the library environment. The problems for investigation are different from one library to another. Problems such as Information needs and use pattern of scientists, Information needs, use pattern and use behaviour of Humanities scholar, use of reference collection in a university library, awareness and use of electronic sources by researchers in Science and Technology etc can be identified as problems for investigation.

ii) Formulation of the objectives

After the selection of the problem, the investigator should formulate the objectives both general and specific in order to study the problem in all its dimensions.

iii)Choice of suitable technique/s or methods

Methods such as direct methods, indirect methods and special and unconventional methods are available for data collection. In the selection of the technique/s due attention should be given to the nature of study and type of the population under study. If the population is large sampling technique can be adopted. The type of sampling technique is selected on the basis of the nature of the population such as homogeneous and heterogeneous. If the population is heterogeneous, stratified sampling technique can be adopted.

iv)Data Collection

In this step data is collected in the form of primary and secondary data from the population by administering the technique/s used in the study. Data may be available in the form of filled up questionnaire, data collected through interview schedule, data collected through observation or data available in the diary etc

v) Analysis and interpretation of the collected data

A detailed analysis of the data is carried out in this step. Statistical analysis can be carried out by using suitable statistical tools. Based on the systematic analysis, necessary interpretations of the study can be arrived at.

vi) Preparation of the report

In the preparation of the final report all principles related to technical writing can be followed. The final report may contain, title of the study, relevance of the study, objectives, methodology, scope and limitations of the study, analysis and discussion, major findings, conclusion etc.

SIGNIFICANCE OF USER STUDIES

User studies have a number of implications on library operations and services. User study has a significant role to play directly or indirectly in rejuvenating a library system and services in the following areas.

1.Collection development

Users play a very significant role in the collection building in a library. The collection should be balanced and suitable to cater to the demands of the user community at the optimum level. In a university library the collection should satisfy the demands of student population, teaching community and researchers. In order to satisfy the demands of this population a librarian should understand users' interests. In a public library the users are with diversified interests. Here also the librarian should be well acquainted with the cross section of the population he has to serve. In a special library the collection should represent the area of specialisation and specialised requirements of the user population. So user studies bring out user interest which is an index in formulating collection building formulae and thereby building up balanced collection in various types of libraries.

2.Weeding out of Books

Today, space for storing documents in libraries especially in older libraries is becoming a serious problem. So it is necessary now to weed out unused books or less used books and keep them as a separate collection. Studies conducted on users based on data collected through issue records, data label etc can be very well used as indices for weeding out books that are unused for a long time or less used books in the library. Thus user studies can help in weeding out unused or less used books and solve space problem in libraries. It is also helpful to bring to light the live collection in the library and separate less used or unused 'dead stock'

3. Resource Allocation

Library user interest has a direct bearing on allocation of resources in a library such as materials, finance, manpower, physical facilities etc. The financial adequacy of a library is measured qualitatively in relation to users' requirements. To quote Gelfand ' commonsense would dictate that standards that are applied arbitrarily and artificially will not impress funding authorities ; budget making and budget justifying must rest upon a firm foundation of local needs that are directly related to the requirements of the library's clientele'. For an objective allocation of resources such as materials, finance, manpower and even physical facilities, users' opinion should be given due weitage.

4. Improvement of Library Techniques

Classification and cataloguing are two important techniques developed by librarians for the organisation of knowledge in libraries. Study of catalogue use in a library will enable to assess the merits and demerits of the physical and internal forms of the catalogue. In the light of the users' opinion suitable modifications or change in the physical form can be made in the catalogue. Modifications or even change of one classification scheme to another scheme, if it is essential can also be possible by conducting appropriate user studies in the field of classification schemes. Besides, before the introduction of new gadgets like computer and other equipments in libraries, users' opinion should be collected for the effective use of the system

5. User- based Information Services

The data evolved from library user study will be a basis to start new services in a library or even to discontinue existing services in the library that are not user-based. Before starting a new service in a library it is essential to ascertain from users whether they require such a service or not. A librarian should not start a service for a minority user community or in achieving his own vested interests. It should be for the benefit of the majority of user community.

6. User Education

Educating a user is very essential for the successful functioning of any system which is new or complex. Today, a modern library is such a system that it demands suitable user education programme for its users. The results of user studies will give a clear idea about the lack of awareness of users in using various types of documents in using certain services and in using some of the tools that are available in the library. These inferences may signify the need for the conduct of appropriate user education in libraries. The importance of user studies for imparting user education programmes has been emphasised in the UNESCO guidelines for the organisation of training courses.

RESEARCH ON USER STUDIES

Research on user studies are becoming more and more interdisciplinary in nature. Studies on user modelling, users' cognitive processes, interface design, research on new research methodologies etc. are certain areas of research on user studies. An attempt towards to formulating a theory of user studies is also on the anvil. Let us hope that the researchers on the various facets of user studies will pave way for the theoretical foundation of user studies.

A number of criticisms are levelled against user studies. They are lack of proper selection of population, limited sample for generalisation, diverse classification of communication channels, lack of proper analysis etc. These criticisms are levelled against earlier studies mainly because proper techniques were not used for the studies. Because of the aforesaid drawbacks information scientists like Britain, Susan Crawford and others doubted the credibility of user studies. But now the situation has changed. Today, the investigators use modern techniques including new statistical tools with the help of computers. Nevertheless, we cannot claim that user studies give full proof results. Errors may occur in the survey mainly due to wrong selection of techniques and samples. Maximum care should be given in the selection of techniques that are suitable to the problems investigated and population studied.

REFERENCES

Britain, JM: Information and its users. Bath, Bath University, 1970.

Cronin, Blaise: Assessing user needs. Aslib Proceedings. 33(2) 1981. P.37-47.

Crawford, Susan: Information needs of user. ARIST.13,1978.

Davis, RA and Bailey: Bibliography of user studies. Philadelphia, Drexel Institute of Technology, 1964.

Fjallbrant, N and Stevenson, M: User education in libraries. London, Clive Bingly.1978.

Gelfand, MA : University libraries for developing countries. Paris, UNESCO, 1968.

Guha, B: Documentation and Information. Calcutta, World Press, 1978.

Kunz, Werner, et al : Methods of analysis and evaluation of information needs. Munchen, Verlag Documentation, 1977.

Lipetz, Ben-Ami: Information needs and users. ARIST.5, 1970.

Paisely, JM: Information needs and uses. ARIST.3, 1968

Ranaganathan, SR: Reference Service. Bombay, Asia publishing, 1961.

Shaw, Ralph: Pilot study on the use of scientific literature by scientists. Washington, National Science Foundation, 1965.

Whittaker, Kenneth: The basis of library based user services. London, LA, 1993.

Wilson, Louis R : The practice of book selection. Chicago, Chicago University Press, 1940

Wilson, TD: Guidelines for developing and implementing a national plan for training and information. Paris, UNESCO, 1968.

Wysoki, A : Study of users' information needs: subject and methods of FID on theoretical problems of informatics. Moscow, All Union Institute for Scientific and Technical Information, 1969.

Chapter

8

Bibliographic Organisation and Control

By bibliographic control we mean the listing of printed and non-printed media in a helpful manner so that it could be easily identified by an information seeker. A reader can get an over all idea on what information resources are at your disposal by creating some sort of list (catalogue or index) of what those information resources are. It is the process of bringing the holdings of a library "under control. James G Olle has defined it as "The effective access to information through information". If all the materials in a subject in all literary or physical forms within a geographical area can be located with the help of the bibliographical tools, then we say that there is full bibliographic control. In fact bibliographic control is the mastery over the printed and published materials by and for the purpose of bibliography. It is synonymous with effective access through bibliographies. While bibliographic organization is the systematic listing of documents. These two concepts are two sides of the same coin that one will not exist without the other.

The main key to what an individual library has the catalogue. Catalogues do not index the individual articles in periodicals, therefore libraries need indexes to provide access to the contents of the journals to which they subscribe. Bibliographic control is formed when we create catalogues and indexes. As Patrick Wilson says, "... if knowledge itself is a form of power, bibliographical control is in a certain sense power over power, power to obtain the knowledge recorded in written form. "Recorded knowledge may in any form and we maintain bibliographic control not only over text but over sound recordings, film, and any other information media.

To have bibliographic control over an item:

- One must know what the item is
- One must have a description of that item
- One must be able to retrieve that record

In a nutshell, we can call this cataloging or indexing, depending simply on whether we are making a catalogue or an index. Generally, we call the file that describes the holdings of a library or group of libraries a catalogue, whereas we call the file that describes the articles in periodicals as index. Both catalogues and indexes organize information for effective retrieval.

A bibliographic record is information that describes a single bibliographic entity. It can be retrieved in various ways. It comprises a description and a set of access points. The steps in cataloging include:

1. Describing the item sufficiently to recognize it and distinguish it from other similar items,
2. Choosing author access points
3. Choosing subject access points

4. Formatting this information for a catalogue
5. Entering the information into a catalogue.

When the bibliographic record is loaded into the catalogue, assuming the catalogue is a computer-based one, the catalogue's software creates indexes of the author entries, the title entries and the subject entries. If the item is a book, a call number enables the patron to go to the shelf that holds the item. If the item is an electronic resource, a hotlink in the record enables the patron to click to the item Charles Ammi Cutter's "Objects" for the catalogue, are, very relevant in the preparation of catalogues and indexes. They are perennial principles to be applied for getting bibliographic control. They are:

1. To enable a person to find a book of which either. the author, the title, the subject is known.
2. To show what a library has by a given author,. on a given subject, in a given kind of literature.
3. To assist in the choice of a book as to its edition (bibliographically), as to its character (literary or topical).

The following points are important for bibliographic control.

1. Completeness: The librarian should have full access to the whole records of a subject.

2. Meticulousness: It should facilitate approach to the specific document unit like parts of a work with multiple contributors and articles in journals etc.

3. Comprehensiveness: By this we mean that it should be exhaustive by including variant forms of documents like print forms, phonographs, databases, CD ROMs etc.

Full bibliographic control is only a utopian idea and can

seldom be achieved. It is natural that a bibliographer can miss out some micro documents untraceably scattered in the vast ocean of literature in various types of documents.

Until 20th century not much attention was paid to bibliographic control for want of financial resources, lack of initiative etc. But by the middle of the 20th century the necessity of bibliographic control was became prominent due to the information explosion in science and technology and social sciences. The competition between nations and among enterprises engaged in industrial, scientific and medical fields also resulted in a flood of published materials.

In 1950 UNESCO organized a conference on improvement of bibliographical services in Paris. This conference urged all the member countries to consider the publication of current national bibliographies. The publication of British National bibliography commenced in 1950. It worked as a fillip to everyone about the importance of bibliographic control. The International Federation of Library Associations and Institutions (IFLA) inaugurated a programme for Universal Bibliographic Control (UBC) in 1974. This was an important landmark in promoting importance of bibliographic control.

The Library of Congress has issued "Bibliographic Control of Web Resources: A Library of Congress Action Plan." The Action Plan consists of themes of the Library of Congress Bicentennial Conference on Bibliographic Control for the New Millennium: Confronting the Challenge of Networked Resources and the Web, held in 2000. The Cataloging Directorate of the Library of Congress convened this invitational conference as a working meeting of experts from the various communities that play a role in the creation, retrieval, and cataloging of Web resources. The primary goals of the Conference were to develop an overall strategy to address the challenges of improved access to Web resources through library catalogues and applications of metadata; and to identify attainable actions for achieving the overall strategy. The aim of the conference, therefore, was to generate recommendations for the Library of Congress, in collaboration with the larger library community, to use as a blueprint for action.

From the content of the recommendations, we arrive at the identification of the following six objectives:

1. Increased availability of standard records for Web resources
2. Enhanced record display and access across multiple systems
3. Collaboration among metadata standards communities for better bibliographic control of Web resources
4. Development of automated tools for harvesting and maintaining metadata
5. Provision of appropriate training for the Web environment
6. Support of research and development to enhance bibliographic control of Web resources. Many of the recommendations would pertain not just to resources available on the World Wide Web, but to digital content available in other venues and even to certain non-digital materials as well.

ACTIVITIES OF NATIONAL AND INTERNATIONAL ORGANISATIONS IN BIBLIOGRAPHIC CONTROL

The following are some of the national and international organizations engaged in the bibliographic organization and control.

National Attempts

An account of national organizations engaged in the bibliographic and documentation activities in India is given under.

National Institute of Science Communication and Information Resources (NISCAIR)

The Indian National Scientific Documentation Centre (INSDOC) was established in 1952 and is based at Sansad Marg in New Delhi. In 2002 it merged with the National Institute of Science Communication (NISCOM) is now known as National Institute of Science Communication and Information Resources (NISCAIR). Both NISCOM and INSDOC, the two premier institutes of the Council of Scientific and Industrial Research (CSIR), were devoted to dissemination and documentation of Science and Technology information. Broadly the core activity of NISCAIR will be to collect/store, publish and disseminate science and technology information through a mix of traditional and modern means, which will benefit different segments of society.

Indian Science Abstracts (ISA) is a semi-monthly abstracting journal which has been reporting scientific work done in India since 1965. Original research articles short communications, review articles, and informative articles published in current scientific and technical periodicals, proceedings of conferences and symposia, monographs and other publications, as well as patents, standards and theses are reported in ISA. ISA is now available online.

The major research and development programmes are design and development of science and technology databases, network-based online services, research and development in information science and technology, foreign language translations, and human resource development in information science and technology.

NISCAIR is also engaged in providing services like electronic mail service, electronic imaging of archival records, compilation of databases and directories, microfilming and slide-making, retrospective conversion of catalogue, bibliographical services and literature search.

NISCAIR conducts an advanced two year post-graduate course in Associateship in Information Science and organizes a number of short-term training courses on computer applications to library and information activities, CDS/ISIS, bibliometrics, information technology, online information retrieval, database management systems and UNIX. NISCAIR prints and publishes publications like Indian Science Abstracts (semi-monthly), Annals of Library Science and Documentation (quarterly) and CSIR Research Output (annual).

The information in Indian Science Abstract is given in classified sequence, each entry providing information about the author including the address of the first author, title and all relevant bibliographic information. Titles in foreign languages are translated into English and the language of the original article is indicated.

Indian Science abstracts includes over 1000 Indian scientific periodicals while it scans about 2000 foreign scientific periodicals for preparing about 36,000 abstracts per annum in twenty four issues. It includes abstracts of original articles, reviews, short communications published in periodicals. Conference proceedings, symposia, monographs and ad hoc scientific publications, patents, standards and theses. Articles of popular nature are not included. It is an exhaustive listing of contributions by Indian scientists and technologists in Indian periodicals and those coming in foreign journals.

National Social Science Documentation Centre(NASSDOC)

The National Social Science Documentation Centre(NASSDOC) is a sub organ under the Indian Council of Social Science Research which is monitoring the research activities in social sciences. It was established in 1970. The primary objective of the NASSDOC is to provide library and information support services to social science researchers. It is considered to be one of the largest repositories of bibliographical databases in the area of social sciences in India.

The ICSSR-NASSDOC library has a rich collection of reference sources like, bibliographies, encyclopedias, doctoral theses, research project reports, books on social science research methodology, computer and information technology, research surveys and also on all social science disciplines.The collection is also augmented by bound volumes of periodicals, current Indian/foreign periodicals including ICSSR publications and other abstracting and indexing journals in social sciences, newsletters and annual reports of different organizations. Government reports/ serials and institutional publications are also acquired on regular basis.

The libray has 5406 Doctoral Theses, 3725 ICSSR funded research projects, 12000 bound volumes of Periodicals and 13615 books. The collection is augmented by 900 current Indian and foreign periodicals. ICSSR also publishes monograph publications and other abstracting and indexing journals in social sciences.Government reports/serials and institutional publications are also acquired on regular basis.

ICSSR-NASSDOC library's membership is open to the following categories of readers. They are Official Members like ICSSR Council members, senior officials of the ICSSR secretariat and regular professional staff of the ICSSR. They are entitled to borrow books from the library. There are also

Institutional Members hip open to autonomous organizations, corporate houses, and research wings of public/private bodies. Institutional or Corporate membership fee is Rs. 4000 per annum. An institutional member can borrow five books at a time for a period of one month.

Consultation membership facility is extended to academicians, research scholars, students and members of general public that may include retired persons and other categories of readers. Borrowing facility is extended to social scientists, academicians, students and general readers who are registered as members of the library. Books are issued against a deposit of Rs.500/- per book. Two books are issued to individual members at a time.

Online Public Access Catalogue (OPAC) is for use by the library members so that subject, author and keyword based searches can be made from the holdings of library books.

NASSDOC's library catalogue is now available online. Members of the library can refer to online bibliographies as well as indexing and abstracting databases to search relevant references on subjects of their study like Econlit, ERIC, International Political Science Abstracts, LISA, Sociological Abstracts, Social Service Abstracts from the NASSDOC library.

Reference queries in the field of social sciences from the scholars are responded to by e-mail, telephone, fax, in person, or through postal correspondence. The scholars are assisted through inter-library loan service and even referred to other institutions to consult material that are not available in their library.

Bibliography on demand is a widely known support service provided by the NASSDOC to social science research community. Normally, the requests for this paid service are received from scholars living in cities and small towns where library and documentation services are severely limited.

Bibliography is a systematic descriptive list of published books, periodical articles, etc as well as unpublished PhD theses and reports on specific subject.

NASSDOC has a very large and rich collection of CD-ROM/on-line based information sources. These are used for searching literature on specific topic on demand. Some of the most used CD-ROM/ and On-line databases in NASSDOC are Dissertation Abstracts on Disc (Humanities and Social Sciences), EconLit, International Political Science Abstracts, Popline, PsycLit, Sociological Abstracts, PsycINFO.

NASSDOC has a programme of acquiring copies of unpublished Ph.D. theses in social sciences accepted by Indian universities. Since 2003 NASSDOC has revised its thesis acquisition policy. It has been decided to pay Rs 1500/- to a scholar for a copy of Ph.D. thesis.

Document delivery service is provided through Inter Library Loan or by photocopying the papers published in periodicals to help the scholars. NASSDOC borrows books, periodicals, reports etc from other libraries to meet the demands of the research scholars. The demand is normally met through inter library loan service. NASSDOC as a member of DELNET (Developing Library Network) can access various databases hosted by the DELNET on its website. NASSDOC can get documents on inter library loan through DELNET from the member libraries.

NASSDOC is involved in creation of databases and information locating tools. Theses tools are available in printed form and some of them are also available on floppies. These are of different type as Library databases, Directories, Indexes, Union Catalogues, Bibliographies, Annotated Index to Indian Social Science Journals, 2005; Bibliographic Data Bank (1), 2005; Bibliographic Data Bank (2), Jan.2002-Dec.2004;Conference Alert July 2005 onwards; Directory of Social Science Research and Training Institutes in India

2005;Directory of Social Scientists in India; ICSSR Research Project Reports, 2000-2005. INSPEL (Indian Social Science Periodical Literature) up to 1970, Online Public Access Catalogue (all the documents available in the NASSDOC library e.g. Books, Theses, Research Reports etc.

NASSDOC provides current awareness service by bringing out different publications at regular intervals. Moreover, photocopies of references included in the CAS publications are provided whenever there is a request for that by the scholars. Ph.D. research scholars get financial assistance from the ICSSR to consult libraries and archives that are located in other cities..

NASSDOC provides financial assistance to conduct research in the field of Library and Information Science and compilation of research/reference tools for social scientists. The project proposals should fall under one of the following categories :

Research in fields like bibliometric analysis, information seeking behavior, library users' study, etc.,compilation of users' guide, directory, annotated bibliography or union catalogue etc,

In order to familiarize the librarians, information intermediaries and social scientists, with new techniques of information technology, NASSDOC organizes short-term training workshops, seminars and lectures on regular basis under its Continuing Education Programme in different parts of the country.

NASSDOC has started microfilming of Ph.D. theses collection. So far approximately 1500 theses have been microfilmed in three phases during 2003 - 2006.. NASSDOC has rich collection of microfilms/microfiches of Ph.D. theses, some of the Indian and foreign journals, Economic Working Papers, Union Catalogues, Government Publications and rare publications. Radio Frequency Identification (RFID) technology has been introduced for inventory management of books and members. This technology obviates the need for human intervention in issuance of books/journals to the members in the Library.

NASSDOC brought out the following products as part of bibliographic organisaiton and control of social science literature

i) Union lists of social science periodicals covering the States of Andhra Pradesh, Maharashtra, Delhi, Karnantaka have been compiled;

ii) Union catalogue of social scince serials. 32 volumes. Giving location about 31,125 serials and periodicals in 550 libraries in 17 States and 2 union teritiries published;

iii) Union catalogue of News papers in Delhi libaries;

iv) Mahatma Gandhi bibliogaphy

v) Retrospective cumulative index of Social scince periodicals.

A number of discipline oriented index volumes covering 240 Indian social science journals have been publised such as :

a) Index to Indian periodicals, Sociology and Psychology

b) Area study bibliographies

c) Indian Education Index

d) Research Information series such as Bibliography on Public Finance, Recent Indian Books on Economics, Political Science, Social and cultural anthropology, Maharashtra - aseelct list, Bihar - a select list etc

e) India in 2000 AD

f) Serial publications such as :Acqusition Update, Quarterly; Current Contents of Indian Social Science Journals Quarterly; Conference Alert Quarterly.

Other Centres

Documentation centres like DESIDOC (Defence Science Documentation Centre) New Delhi, SENDOC(Small Enterprises Documentation Centre) Hyderabad, National Documentation Centre of Mass Communication (NDCMC)etc organise and control literature in the field of defence science, small scale industries and mass communication respectively. National library, Reference Division, Calcutta controls the literture emanated from India through its bibliography, Indian National Bibliography. Indian Association of Special libraries and Information Centres (IASLIC) Calcutta cntrols library and Information Science literature published from India through Indian Library Science Abstract(ILSA). In addition to these activities, research and development organisations, univesities etc are organising and controlling literature by means of bibliographies in India

INTERNATIONAL ORGANISAITONS

International organisations like UNESCO, IFLA, FID etc are some of the major organisations engaged directly or support organisations for bibliographic control and organisation are discussed below.

United Nations Educational, Scientific and Cultural Organisaiton(UNESCO)

The United Nations Educational, Scientific and Cultural Organization (UNESCO) is a specialized agency of the United Nations established in 1945. Its stated purpose is to contribute to peace and security by promoting international collaboration through education, science, and culture in order to promote universal respect for justice, the rule of law, and the human rights along with fundamental freedoms proclaimed in the UN charter. UNESCO has 193 Member States and seven Associate Members. The organization is based in Paris, with over 50 field offices and many specialized institutes and centres throughout the world. Most of the field offices are "cluster" offices covering three or more countries. There are also national and regional offices. UNESCO pursues its objectives through five major programs: education, natural science, social and human sciences, culture, and communication and information. Projects sponsored by UNESCO include literacy, technical, and teacher-training programmes; international science programmes; the promotion of independent media and freedom of the press; regional and cultural history projects, the promotion of cultural diversity; international cooperation agreements to secure the world cultural and natural heritage (World Heritage Sites) and to preserve human rights, and attempts to bridge the worldwide digital divide.

As early as 1942, in wartime, the governments of the European countries, which were confronting Nazi Germany and its allies, met in the United Kingdom for the Conference of Allied Ministers of Education (CAME). The Second World War was far from over, yet those countries were looking for ways and means to reconstruct their systems of education once peace was restored. Very quickly, the project gained momentum and soon took on a universal note. New governments, including that of the United States, decided to join in.

Upon the proposal of CAME, a United Nations Conference for the establishment of an educational and cultural organization (ECO/CONF) was convened in London from 1 to 16 November 1945. After the war it gathered together the representatives of forty-four countries. At the initiative of France and the United Kingdom the delegates decided to create an organization that would embody a genuine culture of peace. In their eyes, the new organization must establish the "intellectual and moral solidarity of mankind" and thereby prevent the outbreak of another world war.

At the end of the conference, thirty-seven countries founded the United Nations Educational, Scientific and Cultural Organization. The Constitution of UNESCO, signed on 16 November 1945, came into force on 4 November 1946 after ratification by twenty countries.

Other major historical factors, as the Cold War, the decolonization process and the dissolution of the USSR, also left their trace on UNESCO. The USSR joined UNESCO in 1954. Nineteen African States became Members in 1960. Twelve Republics from the former Soviet Union joined UNESCO in the period 1991 to 1993.

The General Conference is a gathering of the organization's member states and associate members, in which each state has one vote. Meeting every two years, it sets general policies and defines programmes for the organization.

The Executive Board's 58 members are elected by the General Conference for four-year terms. The Executive Board prepares the sessions of the General Conference and ensures that its instructions are carried out. It also discharges other specific mandates assigned to it by the General Conference. The Secretariat consists of the Director-General and his staff and is responsible for the day-to-day running of the organization..

Considerable reforms were implemented by UNESCO over the past 10 years. The number of divisions in UNESCO was cut in half. At the same time, the number of field units was cut from a peak of 1287 in 1998 to 93 today. Parallel management structures, including 35 Cabinet-level special adviser positions, were abolished. This resulted in substantial saving in expenditure. Open competitive recruitment, results-based appraisal of staff, training of all managers and field rotation were instituted. Regular auditing of accounts is undertaken now. The evaluation of relevance and effectiveness of programmes is carried out to curtail irrelevant and futile activities.

UNESCO is providing international leadership in creating learning societies with educational opportunities for all; it supports research in comparative education; and provides expertise and fosters partnerships to strengthen national educational leadership and the capacity of countries to offer quality education for all.. UNESCO also issues public 'statements' to educate the public: It has several other programmes like endangered language and linguistic diversity projects, water resource management, through the International Hydrological Programme, World Heritage Sites and Maintaining Migration Museums. UNESCO and the Free Software Foundation have jointly funded a free software project for cataloguing.

UNESCO enjoys official relations with 322 international NGOs. Most of these are what UNESCO calls "operational", a select few are "formal" Operational relations are reserved for an NGO with an active presence in the field, with special expertise and with an ability to channel the concerns of their clients. Requests for admission by an NGO to UNESCO for *operational* relations can be made to the Director-General at any time. *Formal* relations are reserved for those NGOs who have a sustained role in cooperating with UNESCO.The highest form of affiliation to UNESCO is "formal associate" and there are 22 of them at present.

There are several UNESCO institutes and centres like UNESCO Institue for Water Education, Delft, UNESCO

International Institute for Educational Planning, Paris Buenos Aires ; UNESCO International Bureau of Education, Geneva, UNESCO European Centre for Higher Education, **Bucarest etc.**

UNESCO 1n 1973 launched the UNISIST programme. It was a conceptual framework and not an operating system. General Informaiton Programme(PGI)was created in 1976 by the merger of UNISIST with programme concerned with the development of documentation, libraries and archives. The major types of activities undertaken by PGI include:

a) Tools for processing and transfer of information.

Under this activity, the following tools are developed.

- Reference Manual for Machine readable bibliographic description.
- Common Communication Format(CCF)
- Reference Manual for Machine -readable descriptions of research projects and institutions
- ISO Standards Handbook.

b) Development of Databases

About 50 projects on creation of databases have been taken up for which assistance regarding software, consultation, equipment and training has been provided. CDS/ISIS software has been developed by UNESCO and is provided free of charge to non-profit organizations in developing countries

c) National Information policies and Infrastructure.

UNESCO has brought out in 1974 the document entitled 'Information policy objectives' in which 113 possible policy objectives are listed.

d) Regional and International cooperative schemes.

Created ASTINFO(Regional Network for the Exchange of Information and Experience in Science and Technology in Asia and the Pacific) and APINESS(Asia-Pacific Information network in Social Sciences)

e) Developing an Information workforce.

Priority has been given for training information professional and users.

International Federation of Library Associations and Institutions(IFLA)

The International Federation of Library Associations and Institutions (IFLA) is the leading international body representing the interests of library and information services and their users. It is the global voice of the library and information profession.

It was founded in Edinburgh, Scotland, in 1927 at an international conference. IFLA now has 1600 Members in approximately 150 countries around the world. IFLA was registered in the Netherlands in 1971. The National Library of the Netherlands, in The Hague, generously provides the facilities for its headquarters.

At its meeting recently, the Governing Board decided to endorse a new model for IFLA's operations, the three pillars, which recognises that IFLA's core functions. This relates to the societal contexts in which libraries and information services operate IFLA's membership and professional matters. These three pillars are supported by the infrastructure offered by the Federation's governance structures, its website and its Headquarters in The Hague.

- The Society Pillar focuses on the role and impact of libraries and information services in society and the contextual issues that condition and constrain the environment in which they operate across the world.

Those issues are addressed currently through FAIFE, CLM, Blue Shield, and World Summit on the Information Society and other arenas.

- The Profession Pillar focuses on the issues covered by the long established Core Activities namely, ALP, ICADS (webmaster: formerly known as ICABS), PAC, UNIMARC and the Sections and Divisions. They lie at the core of its professional practice and help libraries and information services to fulfill their purposes and to shape responses to the needs of clients in a rapidly changing global environment.
- The Members Pillar is very much central to IFLA. It includes the services it offers to members, management of their membership of IFLA, conferences and publications. IFLA 's activities are vibrant and attractive and beneficial for members throughout the world.

Of course, all the three pillars and the underlying infrastructure are interdependent and not mutually exclusive. They offer a way of understanding and presenting IFLA to the library and information sector and to governments and the wider community. The pillars should also provide the framework for IFLA's management and their focus should be reflected in program based budgeting.

The IFLA Statutes were adopted at the IFLA Council meeting in Quebec City, Canada, on 14 August 2008. The text of these IFLA Statutes has been translated into Dutch, and the deed of the amendment of the Statutes of IFLA was executed On 20 **October 2008**, the deed has been signed and the statutes registered with the Chamber of Commerce in The Hague.

IFLA's Governing Board (GB) is responsible for the governance and financial and professional directions of IFLA, and represents the Federation in legal and other formal proceedings.

The Board consists of the President, the President-elect, ten directly elected members, the Chair of the Professional Committee, the Chairs of each IFLA Division, and the Chair of the Management of Library Associations Section's Standing Committee. Three additional GB members may be co-opted to provide expertise or represent special interests. IFLA's Secretary General, who serves as the Board's Secretary, is an ex officio member.

The International Federation of Library Associations and Institutions (IFLA) is the leading international body representing the interests of library and information services and their users. It is the global voice of the library and information profession. IFLA is an independent, international, non-governmental, not-for-profit organization. Its aims are:

- Promote high standards of provision and delivery of library and information services
- Encourage widespread understanding of the value of good library & information services
- Represent the interests of its members throughout the world.

In pursuing these aims IFLA embraces the following core values:

1. The endorsement of the principles of freedom of access to information. ideas and works of imagination and freedom of expression embodied in Article 19 of the Universal Declaration of Human Rights
2. The belief that people, communities and organizations need universal and equitable access to information, ideas and works of imagination for their social,

educational, cultural, democratic and economic well-being

3. The conviction that delivery of high quality library and information services helps guarantee that access
4. The commitment to enable all Members of the Federation to engage in, and benefit from, its activities without regard to citizenship, disability, ethnic origin, gender, geographical location, language, political philosophy, race or religion.

IFLA has two main categories of voting members: Association Members and Institutional Members. Associations of library and information professionals, of library and information services and of educational and research institutes, within the broad field of library and information science, are all welcome as Association Members. Institutional Membership is designed for individual library and information services, and all kinds of organizations in the library and information sector. International organizations in the field of library and information services are entitled to become International Association Members.

More than 25 corporations in the information industry have formed a working relationship with IFLA under Corporate Partners scheme. In return for support they receive a range of benefits including opportunities to present their products and services to IFLA's worldwide membership.

It has Formal Associate Relations with UNESCO, observer status with the United Nations, Associate Status with the International Council of Scientific Unions (ICSU) and observer status with the World Intellectual Property Organization (WIPO) and the International Organization for Standardization (ISO). In 1999, it established observer status with the World Trade Organization (WTO).

IFLA administers a number of Grants and Scholarships to enable aspiring library and information professionals from all over the world to enhance their training and to provide funding for new and exciting projects in the field of librarianship.

IFLA has presently five subject oriented core programmes which intersect the interests and concerns of all libraries and their users, whereever located. The programmes are:

- Universal Bibliographic control and International MARC(UBCIM)
- Universal Availability of Publications (UAP)
- Preservation and Conservation(PAC)
- Universal Data flow and Telecommunications(UDP)
- Advancement of Librarianship in the Third world(ALT)

The professional activities of IFLA are grouped into 8 divisions controlled by a coordinating board. The different divisions with their sections are the following.

vi) General Research libraries.

This division consists of 3 sections that constitute National libraries, University libraries and Parliamentary libraries

ii) Special Libraries

This division constitutes 6 sections that concentrate the activities Government Libraries, Geography and Map Libraries,Biological And Medical Science libraries, Social Science libraries, Science and Technology libraries and Art libraries.

iii) Libraries serving the general public

This division constitutes 6 sections under the areas viz

Public libraries, Libraries serving the disadvantaged persons, Children's libraries, School libraries, Libraries for blind, Library services to multicultural populations.

iv) Bibliographical Control

This division consists of 3 sections such as Cataloguing, Bibliography, Classification and Indexing.

vi) Collections and Services

This division constitutes 5 sections viz Acquisition and Exchange, Interlending and Document Delivery, Serial Publications, Rare Books and Manuscripts, Government Information and Official Publications.

vii) Management and Technology

This division consits of 4 sections such as Conservation, Library Buildings and Equipment, Information Technology and Statistics.

viii) Education and Resarch

This division constitutes 2 sections viz Education and Training, Library Theory and Research.

IFLA offers grants, scholarships and Fellowships to professional in developing countries. IFLA publishes a quarterly journal. Each issue covers news of current IFLA activities and articles, selected to reflect the variety of the international information profession, like freedom of information, preservation, services to the visually impaired and intellectual property. UBC and UAP are two important projects of IFLA.

IFLA also has a publication series. The series deals with many of the means through which libraries, information centres, and information professionals worldwide can formulate their goals, exert their influence as a group, protect their interests, and find solutions to global problems.

There are at present 141 of such publications.IFLA also has a publication series in bibliographical control the latest volume is "National bibliographies in the digital age: Guidance and New Directions."IFLA professional series of publications.is another category of publications. IFLA also offers the following publications free of cost to its members. The publications are: IFLA journal, IFLA Annual, IFLA Trends(Bi-annual report), IFLA medium Term Programme and IFLA status and rules of procedure.

International Federation for Information and Documentation(FID)

The International Federation for Information and Documentation (FID) was created in Brussels in 1895 as the International Institute of Bibliography (IIB) by two Belgians, Paul Otlet (1868-1944) and Henri La Fontaine(1854-1943). It has gone through a number of changes of name that reflect changes of conceptualisation both of the field in which it operates and the way in which it should operate in this field. In 1931 it became the International Institute for Documentation (IID); in 1937 it became the International Federation for Documentation; and in 1988 it became the International Federation for Information and Documentation. It is still known as FID.

The two lawyer friends were inspired by the possibilities for the standardisation of subject coding that they could see in the Decimal Classification. In 1895 they sought the permission of Melvil Dewey to translate the classification and to use it for bibliographical purposes. They had also made the 5x3 inch (125x75 mm) card. This presented to them the possibility of continuous interfiling into a bibliography of entries having a standard format and the easy correction of errors as they were discovered. Otlet and La Fontaine were determined to seek assistance to a universal bibliography under the aegis of a new international organisation. They obtained official patronage for an international conference to consider these matters.

The International Conference on Bibliography assembled in Brussels in 1895. It created an International Institute of Bibliography (IIB) to study matters of classification and the international organisation of bibliography generally. An International Office of Bibliography (OIB), an institutional headquarters for the Institute, was set up as a quasi-official agency of the Belgian government. Its task was to develop a universal bibliography on cards arranged in the classified subject order of the Decimal Classification. Dewey gave Otlet and La Fontaine permission to translate and expand the classification as necessary for bibliographic purposes and agreed to become Vice President of the Institute.

The Universal Bibliographic Repertory, what today is called a database, grew to more than 11 million entries. An international search service, operated through the mails, was set up and led to some analysis of search strategies and the problem of pricing. By 1912 over 1500 requests for information were being received a year.

What became known as the Universal Decimal Classification, a software package used for subject access to the bibliographic and other data bases set up at the OIB, was elaborated by the wide-ranging international collaboration of a large group of scholars. A procedure for number compounding using signs of association and auxiliary schedules was developed, making the UDC the first great faceted classification.

The Bulletin of the Institute was issued from 1895. It is a major journal in which important studies of the Decimal Classification, the theory of what Otlet began to call "Documentation", the international statistics of printing, and the bibliographic applications of microphotography, among a wide range of other matters of bibliographical importance, were reported. The Office of Bibliography also embarked on an ambitious programme of bibliographical publishing.

Two branches of the Institute were opened the Bureau Bibliographique de Paris and the Concilium Bibliographicum in Zurich. The latter was extremely important in developing some of the science divisions of the UDC and in publishing important periodical scientific bibliographies. After 1905 a series of major expansions occurred in the OIB which gradually transformed it into a nucleus of a centre of general internationalism

La Fontaine died in 1943 and Otlet in 1944. It was therefore left to Donker Duyvis to revive the FID after the War. The first post-war conference of FID was held in Paris in 1946 with strong international representation. Most important of all was the close relations that were at once set up with UNESCO. E.J. Carter, the Head of the Libraries Section, encouraged FID to apply for grants for various tasks. He also encouraged FID and IFLA to consider their relationship and possible avenues of cooperation.

Donker Duyvis retired in 1959. Like Otlet before him, he had also rendered great service in leading the activities of FID. He deployed the meager resources of the institution very wisely during his tenure of office. Not surprisingly the UDC remained a primary concern. He had no obvious successor and the organisation was confronted with all the usual issues of stability.

The modern history of the FID will require a study of its formal structure as reflected in the periodic revision of its statutes, beginning with those adopted in 1948. It has had to struggle with questions of changing purpose and function. These received priority in long term plans and other formal planning documents. The creation of the regional commissions (for Latin America and Oceania) and the achievements possible through them is a landmark in the history of the FID. The post-war presidents were powerful and influential personalities. Most of them undertook planning and other exercises that directed the destiny of FID in the right direction

The UDC in spite of its popularity, is still an imperfect tool of information management and control.. FID has gradually been accredited to a great many inter-governmental organisations, the earliest and most important of which is UNESCO. It has obtained observer status or formal membership in a number of non-governmental organisations. Some of these, especially the International Federation of International Associations, act in fields closely related to those of the FID. This presents interesting questions of how FID's mission and its international support have been negotiated both internally and externally. It is one of the longest lived non governmental organisations and as such presents important historical challenges.

Activities and Functions of FID

The activities and functions include i) Conference and seminars are conducted regularly so as to give information professionals an opportunity to discuss issues pertinent to their development and to highlight development in the information field. ii) Active publication programme : FID has published a number of publications such as FID News Bulletin, Document delivery survey, a regular insert in FID News Bulletin, Internatinal Forum on Information and Documentation, International Financial legislaton bulletin, FID directory, FID annual report, projects etc.

In order to carry out various programmes, FID has appointed the following Commisions, Committees and Special subject interest groups.

FID Commissions

FID/CAF Commision for Western, Eastern and Sothern Africa.

FID/CAO Commission for Asia and Oceania

FID/CLA Commission for Latin America

FID/NANE Commission for Northern Africa and the Near East

FID/ ROE Commission for Regional Organisation for Europe.

FID Committes

FID/CR Classification Research

FID/ET Education and Training

FID/II Infrmation for Industry

FID/IP Information Policis and Programmes

FID/IPI Intellectual Property Issues

FID/ LI Lingustics in Information

FID/SD Social Science Documentation and Information

FID/UDC Universal Classiciation Consortium

Special Interest Groups

FID/ASME Advisory Services for Small and Medium sized Enterprises

FID/BFI Banking, Finance and Insurance Information

FID/EIS Executive Information System

FID/MIP Roles, Careers and development of the Modern Information Professional

FID/MSS Marketing of Systems and Services

FID/SCRM Saftey Control and Risk Management

FID/TIRM Training for Information Resource Managemnt

FID/EI Environmental Information

FID/IT Information Technology

FID/IPA Informaiton for Public Administration.

REFERENCES

Bhatt, R.K: Information systems. New Delhi, Pragati Publications,2009.

Bourne, R: IFLA International programme for UBC. IFLA journal.12, 1986.pp.341-43.

Guichat, G and Monou, M: General introduction to the techniques of information and documentation work. Paris, UNESCO, 1983.

Gupta, BM and Jain,VK,Ed: Handbook of Libraries, Archives and Information cenres in India.Vol.8, Delhi, Aditya Prakashan,1985.

Kumar, PSG: Information sources and services: Theory and practice.Delhi, B.R Publishing, 2004

Chapter

9

Information Services

The concept of information service as we understand today is a twentieth century phenomenon. This was applied predominantly by special libraries especially in Science and technology libraries. Harrod's Librarians' Glossary defines information service as 'a service provided by, or for, a special library which draws attention to information possessed in the library or information department in anticipation of demand. In the context of library the function of information service is an activity to find out what is already known on a particular subject or topic and make it available to the reader. Therefore to make libraries effective and useful, the librarians and information managers need to be well informed of the latest developments in the universe of knowledge to satisfy the information needs of users.

Today, information is considered as an important resource for overall development of the society. It is impossible to acquire knowledge without information. It is used by the various types of user population for various purposes. Students' community need information for learning according to the syllabi and curriculum. The teachers are in need of information to teach, scientists and researchers need to get the information for their research and new invention incessantly. The need of the scientists and researchers is limited but multidimensional while others' need is more popular and decentralised.

There are a number of reasons that demand for need based information services from the libraries and information centres in the present day information environment. They include: i) Quantitative growth of literature; ii) Multiplicity of languages; iii) Intellectual awareness and updating; iv) Research and development; v)Industrial and commercial need etc.

PHILOSOPHY OF INFORMATION SERVICE

There are two approaches or philosophies that can be followed in providing information services to readers. In fact, certain services can be given anticipating that these services are beneficial to the users. These types of services are known as anticipatory services. The aim of this approach is to keep the users abreast with the current developments in their fields. Services such as documentation service, current awareness services etc can be grouped under this category. While certain services are provided on demand or based on the specific request of the users. These types of services are known as responsive services. Services such as reference service, referral service, translation service, reprographic services, bibliographical services, information consolidation products services etc are grouped under this category.

A discussion of the various types of services is given below.

DOCUMENTATION

The word 'documentation' came into use with beginning of 20th century. Documentation actually means much more than building bibliography of micro documents. It surpasses the technique of providing bibliographical and reference service. The importance of documentation lies in the provision of information to the specialists with emphasis on nascent micro thoughts that are really carriers of research output.

According to Bradford, documentation is the 'process of collecting and subject classifying all the records of new observations and making them available, at need, to the discoverer or inventor. Harrod's Librarians' Glossary defines documentation as 'the study of the acquisition, handling, and communication of information, particularly relating to scientific reports, semi-published material, statistics etc' While ASLIB adopted the definition in connection with the publication of ' Journal of Documentation' as 'recording, organising and dissemination of specialised knowledge. In other words documentation means collecting, organising and providing micro-thought to the scientists and research scholars' According to Encyclopaedia of Library and Information Science, 'documentation does, in fact, embrace the whole gamut of operations from the discovery or creation of new knowledge, through its publication, analysis, classification and arrangement to its arrival at the user, that is to say, report writing, publication, analysis, classification indexing reassembly, presentation and dissemination' Dr. S.R Ranganathan defines 'documentation as 'promotion and practice of bringing the nascent micro-subjects into use by specialists, pin pointedly, exhaustively and expeditiously, in spite of the ever increasing cascade of specialised nascent micro subjects communicated through an ever multiplying number of micro documents'. He has correlated all the significant concepts in the definition of documentation in conformity with Five Laws of Library Science.

Need of Documentation

There are a number of socio-economic and cultural environments in the information world that prompted librarians to start documentation as a need-based new speciality service in libraries. They are :

1. Quantitative growth of Literature : In the ancient times literature was produced only in limited numbers. But, after the scientific renaissance quite a lot of literature produced all over the world. Hence 20th century witnessed exponential growth of literature that resulted information explosion or information deluge. In this information environment users of information found very difficult to access and retrieve information from the large quantum of literature. This necessitated starting of documentation service from libraries.

2. Economic Issues : No library or information centre in the world can claim self sufficient in respect of financé. Every library has its limited financial resources and cannot procure all publications. Under these circumstances researchers may find problems to complete research projects. This problem can be solved by introducing documentation service.

3. For research work : Research and development activities are significant input for a national development in all spheres of human activities. Hence for a meaningful research, nascent micro-thought carrying new born information is very essential especially in an age of information explosion. In such a situation, services such as documentation enable to filter large quantum of information and channelise pin pointed information to the researchers with precision.

4. Social needs : Dr. S.R. Ranganathan has stated that the need of documentation is due to social need. In yester years the research work was depended on the need of researcher but now it is a social need. Increasing population and to satisfy the increasing need documentation is quite necessary. At present industrial productivity and research projects depend up on documentation

5. Problems of Communication : In early days, the research works were relatively less in quantity and users were less and there was no problem in communication. But now there is a rapid growth in literature on one side and increased research output on the other side witnessed difficulty in communication. Documentation service would enable to bridge the gap in communication between the reader and the research output

6. Organisation of Literature : Organisations like trade, commerce and industry and other research institutions specialising in specific subject give importance to specific and specialised literature rather than traditional literature. To collect, organise and disseminate the latest developments to the researchers, executives etc, documentation is warranted.

7. Industrial Needs : Industrial development is growing in a rapid pace. Right information is essential to enhance productivity and profit and to economise cost factor. Every day new techniques and mechanised devices are being used. To do these jobs effectively and efficiently, libraries attached to industrial units should provide documentation service.

8. Language Barrier : Today the world literature is published in a number of languages including national and regional languages. It is quite impossible to any scientist to study all languages and read the published literature in his/her field of specialisation. In order to overcome the language barrier confronted by the users documentation service can be introduced.

Objectives of Documentation

Documentation has vital role in the present day information environment for its research and development. The following are the major objectives of documentation

i) There is a high speed in literature explosion which cannot be controlled without the help of documentation;

ii) Scientists and researchers cannot afford to search as well as specialise the literature simultaneously, documentation helps them to meet their needs promptly;

iii) Updateness of intellectual awareness cannot be attained without documentation;

iv) In order to increase production which is a dire need of industry and commerce documentation is imperative;

v) It is very essential to collect, classify and distribute all types of documents related with human activities of all fields;

vi) To collect, organise and distribute the micro thought to the scientists and researchers;

vii) Book selection, receipts, accession, classification, cataloguing, circulation of books are the main activities of libraries which can be easily done with the help of documentation.

Facets of Documentation

According to Dr. S.R Ranganathan, documentation consists of the following facets or components.

- Documentation work

- Documentation Service
- Liaison work

The facet, documentation work, is otherwise known as active documentation and documentation service is otherwise known as passive documentation. The major activity in the documentation work facet is the preparation of documentation list while the major work involved in the documentation service facet is the distribution or supply of the documentation list. Documentation list is a list of those documents which are listed at one place for specific objective. Dr. S.Ranganathan has defined documentation list as the new name of bibliography which includes micro thought related documents, research, business, administration of subject experts of their own field

The facet, liaison work consists of i) arrangement for translation service where necessary; ii) arrangement for the supply of reprographic copies of documents when the research worker desires to own them; and iii) procurement for a research worker copies or reprographic copies of documents not available in the library, from other libraries within the country or outside.

REFERRAL SERVICE

Since no library can be self sufficient as far as its information resources are concerned, it should be able to direct enquires which it cannot answer to other institutions or individuals who may be able to provide appropriate answers. This service is called referral service. This service does not provide the user with the documents or information needed for his query but refer him to the sources such as secondary publications, information units, professional organisations, research institutes, specialists etc tell him where to find them. They use union catalogues, directories, files on sources, if necessary specially created for the purpose. It is difficult for them to gauge their effectiveness unless they keep in close touch with their sources and users, a task that is easier when they serve a small geographical area. When they exceed a certain size, they have to be organized as a separate section of the library since the need to keep the files on sources up to date become rather time consuming.

An information centre that provides referral service is known as referral centre. Harrod's Librarians' Glossary defines referral centre as 'An organisation for directing researchers for information and data to appropriate sources such as libraries, agencies, documentation centres and individuals. The functions of the referral centre are:

i) To collect on a world-wide basis information about data/information sources within the subject or mission.

ii) To prepare a comprehensive inventory of the types of information /data services available from these sources with a detailed subject index to facilitate its access.

iii) To guide users to the appropriate sources where from the required data or information may be obtained.

iv) To function as an intermediary between enquirer and the organisation and /or individuals who possess specialised knowledge on the subject of enquiry.

CURRENT AWARENESS SERVICES

Current awareness service connotes being well informed over wide areas going beyond the fields which are obviously and directly relevant to current activities. Harrod's Librarians' Glossary defines current awareness service as 'a system, and often a publication, for notifying current documents to users of libraries and information services'

Current awareness services (CAS) are devices meant for the speedy announcement of newly acquired information or documents. Timeliness is the essence of this service, and it is therefore also called as an alerting mechanism. The main objective of this service is to keep the research, development and management personal of the organisation and other interested organisations abreast of the current developments in their respective fields of specialisation as quickly as possible. Current awareness services are to be designed with the main emphasis on speed of announcement, ease of use, and minimum time required for compilation work. In fact, current awareness service is a device of an information system through which all users of information can be informed promptly as soon as possible after publication but before absorption into the secondary documents, of current literature selected from broad subject field or on an area in which a group of persons are interested, and presented in a manner, volume and rhythm intended to facilitate or cultivate current approach to information.

Characteristics of Current Awareness Service

The characteristics of current awareness services are:

- The service is usually in the form of a publication, and attempts to bring information that is current or new or of recent origin to the attention of its users;
- The service does not seek to answer any specific questions that the user may have;
- The service is usually confined to a well defined subject area or topic ;
- The service may sometimes confine itself to a given type of literature ;

- The service could be bibliographical in nature;
- The service endeavours to alert its users to recent development or news as quickly as possible; and
- The service attempts to make browsing convenient and easy for the user.

Types of Current Awareness Services

The current awareness services can be broadly categorised into two types. They are:

- Those services which are directed towards all users; and
- Those services which are directed towards individuals or group of users.

There are various types of current awareness services which can be directed towards all types of users without any discrimination of their areas of interest. They are:

i) Addition list or Accession list

This is a rudimentary form of current awareness service. This is a list of latest additions or accessioned documents compiled in a library. This list is usually brought out as a current awareness tool presuming the fact that the list contains latest publications in various subject areas acquired by a library.

ii) Bibliographical services

A series of services can be provided to the users in the form of adhoc bibliographies in specialised areas, indexing and abstracting services etc focussed on the micro documents recently acquired in a library. These types of services can be developed internally by each library. These types of services are also produced externally in large numbers by various agencies. Indian Science Abstract, CAS,

BIOSIS, LISA etc INDEX MEDICUS etc are some of the such services.

iii) Contents pages of Journals

This type of service can be generated as an in house one. Photo copies of the contents pages can be taken of all or some of the journals received by a library as they arrive. These copies can be systematically arranged alphabetically on the basis of the title of journal and then circulated to users. Contents pages of journals are also published by commercial agency Institute for Scientific Information(ISI) Philadelphia. The Current Contents - Physical Sciences, published weekly reproduces the contents pages of over 700 journals and The Current Contents- Life Sciences and Chemical Sciences etc are some of the examples.

iv) News Paper Clipping Service

News papers are current information media. They publish news of current happenings on the political, social, economic, scientific, cultural fields etc. Important information pertaining to certain subjects areas that are of institutional interest may be published in the news papers. Such information may be scanned and important items may be cut from the news papers and brought the same under the notice of the users. This type of service is usually provided in special libraries.

v) Library Bulletin

Library bulletin may be in the form of a news bulletin generated from libraries giving items of current general information or a list of recent addition, list of contents of journals, indexes and abstracts, bibliographical survey, research studies completed, research in progress etc or combination of these. The scope of the bulletin depends upon the needs of the organisation and the resources made available to the information centre or library.

vi) Routing of Periodicals

Routing of periodicals is an important means of dissemination of current information. In special libraries or information centres the back volumes of periodicals are circulated while the current periodicals are routed. There are two types of routing that can be followed viz radial routing and circular routing. In the radial routing the library sends the periodical to the first person on the list, who returns it to the library. Then the library sends the periodical to the second person in the list, third person, so on. In the circular routing, the library sends the current issue of the journal to the first person on the list, who passes it on to the next name in the list, ultimately the last person in the list returns it to the library.

SELECTIVE DISSEMINATION OF INFORMATION (SDI)

Selective dissemination of information (SDI) is based on the concept of personal service. It is one of those services which are directed towards individuals so as to cater to individual requirements. It is a refinement of current awareness service. In fact it is an intensified personal service and it differs from other types of current awareness services in this respect. This idea was conceived by H.P Luhn in 1961. According to Luhn 'SDI is that service within an organisation which concerns itself with channelling of new item of information from various sources to those points within the organisation where they can usefully serve someone's interest. It endeavours to prevent indiscriminate distribution of new information and avert the resulting danger of not communicating at all' In fact SDI is a type of current awareness service which, under optimum conditions involves a screening of document, selecting information exactly tailored to meet the specific needs of each user or group of users and supplying the information directly to exact individual or group of users. Its objective is to keep users of the system informed of the developments in their respective fields of interest without deluging them with irrelevant and unwanted documents.

A computerised SDI system comprises the following steps'

- Construction of users' profile
- Construction of document profile
- Matching mechanism
- Issue of notification
- Feedback from users
- Modification of the users' profile, if needed.

Construction of Users' Profile

The first step consists of creating profile of the users who are to be given SDI service. A profile consists of key words that collectively characterise the subject interest of the individual or organisation. The aim of creating profiles is to define the topics of interest appropriately. Gathering of information for a profile is an important step. A proforma is designed for the purpose. A user is requested to fill up the proforma. The proforma should include the information such as name of the user, qualifications, status, phone number, name of the institution, address, area of specialisation and key words, languages known etc. In the selection of the areas of interest and key words controlled vocabulary tools should be used so as to avoid noise in matching of the user profile with document profile. The collected user profiles should form an input in the computer.

Construction of Documents Profile

This step involves the construction of database of the documents. This can be created internally based on newly added documents in the library. Each document received by the library or information centre is scanned, indexed and abstracted. Proper subject analysis of the document is extremely important for the success of the SDI service. The same controlled vocabulary used for the preparation of the key words for representing subject interest in the users' profile should be used for selecting Key words for representing the subject of the document in the documents profile for correct matching.

Externally created databases can also be used for SDI service. When an external database is used for SDI service, often it has to be reformatted through a conversion programme to achieve compatibility with the local system. The document profiles form another input in the computer system.

Matching Mechanism

In the matching mechanism, at a predetermined stage the computer match two inputs viz users' profile with document's profile by a programme. This matching process produces output as notification.

Issue of Notification

The output is printed by the system in the form of two cards. One card is known as 'information card' which contains details about documents or information itself matched for the specific user by the system.. Another card is known as response card which contains information to be furnished by the user and return to the library as a feedback mechanism to ascertain the degree of usefulness of information retrieved.

Profile Modification

In the process of going through the notifications, a user may indicate the usefulness of the documents disseminated to him/her or point out that output provided in the information card was relevant or partially relevant or not at all relevant. At this stage, the SDI system is to modify the particular profile in case the user opines that the information was not relevant or partially relevant. This implies that modification of the users profile is guided largely by the feedback provided by the user. The SDI system operations analyse the reasons for the dissemination of the items that were not found relevant. This could result in the revision or modification of the users' profile or search expressions for the user. Modification of the user profile can be done with discussion with the user. The modified profiles' performance is again monitored to ensure that it is better than the earlier profile.

BACKUP SERVICES

Reprographic and translation services are categorised as auxiliary services or backup services. These are considered as tailor made services or supporting services to documentation.

REPROGRAPHIC SERVICES

The art and method of document reproduction generally defined as reprographic methods have come to stay as a basic necessity in every aspect of modern life, more so in the field of communication and dissemination of information. Reprography is a term used to refer to photocopying as well as duplicating documents whereby one or more copies of the same size or in reduced or enlarged form are produced.

The advantages of reprography have found innumerable applications in libraries and their scope is particularly unlimited. The major advantages are:

i) Procuring copies of out-of print materials or unpublished works;

ii) Securing the contents of valuable documents;

iii) Publications in limited editions;

iv) Saving storage space ;

v) Acquisition of copies of portions of books, periodicals etc with out acquire the whole of the original etc.

Methods of Reprography

The following methods of reprography are in vogue. They are : i)Copying process and techniques; ii)Duplicating process and techniques; and iii) Micrographic process and techniques

Copying process and techniques enables librarians to have photocopies of any size, enlarged, reduced or full size. By this method copies of an original document can be made quickly and economically. There are a number of process available for making copies. They include a) Electronic process; b) Diazo graphic process; c) Thermo graphic process; d) Silver halide process.

By the method of duplicating process and techniques a large number of copies of a document are produced quickly and economically. The various techniques of duplicating process are : i) Offset duplication; ii) Stencil duplication; and iii)Spirit duplication'

The micro graphic process and techniques may be described as miniaturisation of document. In this method documents are highly reduced in size and recorded on microform for saving storage space and handling convenience. These microforms of documents include microfilm, microfiche, ultra fiche, micro cards, aperture cards, microfilm cartridges, microfilm cassettes, jacket, computer output microfilm etc.

With the very wide range of reprographic systems and equipment available, the proper selection of document copying process and equipments for any establishment depends upon a number of considerations. In every case, the full requirement of the organisation has to be examined and compared with the capabilities of the various techniques / equipments in order to decide upon the most suitable process and equipment. Some of the considerations which would determine the choice are cost, number of copies required, quality of reproduction, durability. size of the copy, type of original and colour etc.

TRANSLATION SERVICE

Translation service is also considered as a back up service or supporting service. Mostly researchers and scientists are anxious to read primary sources for their research work. Sometimes documents are in such a language script from which the researcher is not familiar with the language. To overcome such language barriers and make use of such documents translation services are needed.

The non-English portion of world's scientific and technical literature required by scientists, engineers and technologists probably amounts to as much as 50%, an estimate by the National lending library of Great Britain. At present, the most expedient way to make this body of foreign language material available to the scientists and engineers of the system is by the provision of translation facility. Translation from German, French, Russian, Danish, Japanese etc to English would be necessary. No one is expected to have proficiency in more than one or two languages, and unless some effective mechanism is created after getting over, language barrier, no researcher can have totality of information in his field of specialisation.

Types of Translations

Translation may be divided into the following two categories.

i) **Adhoc translation:** This type of translation is the selective translation of the articles published in literature; and

ii) **Cover to cover translation:** In this method every word of the material is being translated into the target language.

Scope of Technical Translation

The technical translation activity would have the following objectives:

i) Establishment of a translation abstracting service

ii) Provision of an adequate responsive and anticipatory translation service.

iii) Maintenance of translation bank.

iv) Cover to cover translation of selected journals.

v) In service training for building up a cadre of highly skilled specialised translators.

vi) Establishment of cooperation and coordination with international information systems.

Translation Services

Translation work by its very nature is extremely expensive and time consuming. A good subject knowledge coupled with fluency in both source and target languages is a rare combination. This has prompted all those who are interested in translation work to seek mutual help and cooperation. This has resulted in the establishment of national and international centres of translations.

National Organisations

In India, the following organisations are actively engaged in the translation activities in the field of Science and Technology, Humanities and Social Sciences.

In Science and Technology fields, many governmental and public undertaking organisations such as ONGC,BARC, BHEL, MECON, HAL, RITES, DRDO have their own translation facilities to meet their own requirements from a limited number of languages. NISCAIR, IASLIC, DESIDOC etc also provide translation services.

In the field of Humanities and Social Sciences in India the following agencies are engaged in the translation service activities. These include:

i) National Council of Educational Research & Training (NCERT) and National Book Trust(NBT) are engaged in translation of textbooks into various Indian languages

ii) The Central Institute of English and Foreign languages, Hyderabad and the Institute of Asian Studies, Madras conduct language courses and perform translation activities.

iii) The School of Foreign languages (SFL), Delhi conducts courses in Chinese, Japanese, Russian, French and German languages for defence personnel and sponsored candidates. The school undertakes translation work on demand.

iv) Indian Council of Cultural Relations, Delhi does literary translations to project Indian culture and Indian national personalities and leaders.

International Organisations

At the international level, certain organisations are engaged in the translation activities as international pools or international translation banks. They are:

1. National Translational Centre (NTC): It is located at the John Crear library, Chicago organised in 1953. It is a cooperative non-profit translation pool and its services are designed to eliminate costly duplication of translation efforts and to provide free funds for translating new materials. Translations available from the NTC are also available from the BLLD of Great Britain on loan or in photocopy.

2. International Translation Centre(ITC) : The centre came into existence in 1960 under its former name the European Translation Centre (ETC). The present name was adopted in 1975. ITC is located in Delft, Netherlands. The main aim of this centre is to act as an instrument for the exchange of information by means of translation and prevention of duplication of translation work.

Federation of International des Traducturs(FIT) located at Belgium, International Association of Conference Interpretes, Geneva, Switzerland, International Association of Conference Translators at Vaud, Switzerland, INFOTERM, Vienna, Austria etc are also other important international centres of translations.

Publications

The following are some of the translation services or publications generated as tools for bibliographic control by various international agencies in translations. They are i) World Translation Index published by International Translation Centre; ii) Translation Register Index published by SLA Translation Centre; iii) Translation Bulletin, a monthly publication of the Commission of the European Committees and Centre National de la Recharche scientifique, France,; iv) Cumulative Index to English Translations ; v) Common wealth Index of unpublished translations by the Library Association, London etc

REFERENCES

Atherton,P: Handbook of Information systems and services. Paris, UNESCO, 1977

Dhiman, Anil K and Yashoda Rani: Learn information and reference sources and services. New Delhi, ESS ESS,2005

Foskett, DJ: Information service in libraries. Ed.2.Connecticut, Archon Books, 1967'

Krishan Kumar. Reference service. New Delhi, Vikas,2008.

Kumar, PSG: Information sources and services: Theory and practice. New Delhi, BR Publishing Corporation, 2004.

Luhn, HP: selective dissemination of new scientific information with the aid of electronic processing equipment. American Documentation.12(1) 1961.

Prytherch, Ray,Comp: Harrod' Librarians' Glossary.. England, Gower, 1995.

Weisman, HM: Information systems, services and centres. New York, Becker, 1972

Chapter

10

Information Systems and Products

Due to the unabated and geometric proportion of growth in knowledge numerous information systems or data bases have come up. The advancements in information, communication and computer technology have rendered them accessible online to everyone through computerized networks. In printed databases there is a limitation to include a particular subject heading, but in a computerised systems a single document can be included under several subject facets of the document. With a minimal search time these databases can be used for compilation of bibliographies, current awareness services and retrospective literature search. Today there are many full text databases and that trend is on the increase. There are hundreds of databases now and most of them are oriented for the specialists in various subject areas viz Medical Science, Chemistry and Chemical technology, Biological sciences, Agricultural Science, Nuclear Science, Development Science etc..

INFORMATION SYSTEM

Information system is an organized procedure for collecting, processing, storing, and retrieving information to satisfy a variety of needs. It has been conceived as a set of interrelated components that jointly switch information from producers to users, following identical or compatible rules and procedures with a view to world-wide exchange and interconnections. From the functional point of view, UNISIST defines that 'Unique integration of men, methods, organizational patterns, software elements whose coordinated operations provide manifold dispersed communities of users with all the input data relevant to them at any time, irrespective of origin or physical location, in a variety of possible output formats selected by them as best suited to their information gathering habits, abilities and requirements'

A well- developed information system helps in identifying the research gaps for developing methodology and transfer of technology. It is also a proven instrument to regulate information explosion, multiplicity of data, new thrusts in educational programmes etc in the present day information management environment. Samuelson has given the following overall objectives of an information system.

i) To render, as best possible, library and information services to all those who are identified;

ii) To make sure that the educationists and persons who are engaged in research and development get information for the development of high quality education;

iii) To allow for better use of the existing research and development in the country;

iv) To improve the practical utilization of the results of foreign methodology and contents.

Pauline Atherton has stated the following objectives for an information system.

- To study users' needs as a basis for evaluation and design of an information system ;
- To provide access to recorded materials;
- To select and acquire those information resources as are needed to support research in any sector;
- To respond to request for data ;
- To provide inter-library loan faster.

Information systems are divided into National information system and International systems based on the purview of the area covered. Information system is also categorized into Discipline oriented system and Mission-oriented systems. Discipline oriented system is related to specific subjects like Mathematics. Biology, Chemistry, Physics, Economics etc (e.g.CAS, BIOSIS etc) while Mission oriented system relates to professional groups without any demarcation among disciplines (e.g INIS, AGRIS etc)

In this chapter an attempt is made to give an account of National and International information systems and their, objectives, structure, activities, services and information products.

NATIONAL INFORMATION SYSTEM FOR SCIENCE AND TECHNOLOGY (NISSAT)

The increasing role of science and technology in the economic and social development of the country generated a pressing demand for faster technology transfer to the industries. In fact information centres serving the needs of different industries and R & D units, had to be coordinated and organized into an integrated system. This helps to avoid duplication of activities and to conform to national and international standards. In order to meet this requirement the National Information System for Science & Technology(NISSAT) was launched in 1977. Besides establishing the internal linkages between the information industry, its promoters and users, NISSAT also made efforts to establish a bridge between information resource developers and users in India and other countries. The broad objectives of NISSAT are:

1. Development of national information services
2. Promotion of existing information systems & services
3. Introduction of modern information handling tools & techniques
4. Promotion of international cooperation in information
5. Development of indigenous products & services
6. Organization of skill development programmes
7. Promotion of R & D in Information Science & Technology

Subject Coverage

The NISSAT programmes had the mandate to cover the entire spectrum of science and technology. However, special care was taken not to dwell upon subjects already being handled by other national programmes. NISSAT also sought the expert views of institutions and individuals working on a given subject or its allied areas. It also promotes the library movement in the country through the introduction of modern information technology, tools and techniques.

Main Functions

The main functions of NISSAT are:

1. Strengthening of information services through Information Centres in Science and Technology, Value

rural areas, organize these in a multimedia database, translate the information in local languages and disseminate down to the masses.

NACIDS: National Access Centres to International Database Services

NISSAT established eleven NACIDS facilities in Ahmedabad, Bangalore, Calcutta,Chennai, Delhi, Hyderabad, Mumbai, Pune, Thiruvananthapuram, Guwahati and Bhopal for providing online facility to access international database services. The NACIDS provide search services from Dialog and STN databases. The centres are gaining popularity in spite of the fact that the users have to pay the full cost of a search.

National Server on Factual Science and Technology Information

The project is intended to collect and collate factual information from diverse sources, and host these on a server christened VIGYAN http://www.vigyan.org.in*h* or *http://144.16.72.160*) for national and international access.

Several National websites are being created for national and international access. Intellectual Property Rights (http://www.iprlawindia.org),. Knowledge Management (http://www.kmindia.org),. Indian Tea (http://www.indian *tea.org*) etc. are some of the websites.

NISSAT also supports the Indian effort Vidyanidhi to list the full text of various types of theses materials and establish the procedure for treatment. The materials will be web-enabled for wider access. The technology will be transferred to various Ph D awarding agencies for information handling and dissemination in a distributed mode. NISSAT encourages indigenous database development activities and has NISSAT completed 11 database development projects such as

Directory of manufacture of various kinds of Ferrous and Non- Ferrous and Special Castings, Biographical database of Indian Scientists, Indian Sugar Industry, Directory of Libraries and Information Centres in Gujarat, databases on Virus and Virology etc.

NISSAT has taken initiatives for promoting resource-sharing activities through Library Networks in Calcutta, Delhi, Mumbai, Pune, Ahmedabad and Mysore. These initiatives are aimed at ensuring better utilization of S&T information resources I T Applications

Since the inception, NISSAT had accorded high priority to all aspects of computer based bibliographic information processing. As part of the programme NISSAT acquired proven software packages like CDS/ISIS. NISSAT subsequently obtained the official rights for distribution of the CDS/ISIS for bibliographic information processing and retrieval and IDAMS for statistical data processing from UNESCO.

SANJAY is a package developed by NISSAT to help the libraries and information centres in India to improve their housekeeping and service functions through automation. The package is totally menu driven and can be used even by non-professionals. The package was released for marketing in September 1995. It also brings out a quarterly newsletter.

INTERNATIONAL INFORMATION SYSTEMS FOR THE AGRICULTURAL SCIENCES AND TECHNOLOGY (AGRIS)

AGRIS is the International Information System for the Agricultural Sciences and Technology of the Food and Agricultural Organization of the United Nations. It started in 1974. More than one hundred countries are participating in the compilation of this and is a very authoritative index. It facilitates free exchange of information bringing together agriculture-related literature. The AGRIS metadata corpus was developed to allow its users to have free access to knowledge available in agricultural science and technology. AGRIS was developed to be an international cooperative system to serve both developed and developing countries..There are 2.5 million structured bibliographic metadata records on agricultural science and technology publications collected during the last 35 years since 1975 dealing with all aspects of agriculture including forestry, fisheries, human nutrition and environment.

AGRIS aims to ensure that, the resources contained in repositories located in several regions be available to the general user, with few restrictions. Access to the AGRIS Repository is provided through the AGRIS Search Engine that enables retrieval of bibliographic records contained in the AGRIS Repository and allows users to perform either full-text or brief queries.

Data indexing in AGRIS is based on the AGROVOC thesaurus. AGROVOC is a comprehensive multilingual agriculture thesaurus that was developed with the cooperation of FAO member countries. It is used for indexing data in agricultural information systems and is updated continuously. The first version of AGROVOC was produced in 1982. It is available in English and several other languages including Hindi. All types of documents like monographs, journal articles. conference papers reports, dissertations, patents, slides, electronic media etc. are included in the AGRIS databases. The majority of them are journal articles. Each document contains details like title in English and original language, authors and their affiliation, publication source and identification, subject category codes, abstracts in English, French and Spanish etc.

AGRIS is a cooperative system in which participating countries input references to the literature/documents produced within their boundaries and, in return, draw on the information provided by the other participants. The bibliographic references forwarded by participating countries are collected and processed in the AGRIS Processing Unit in Vienna. To date 159 national and 31 international and intergovernmental centres participate and submit about 14.000 items per month. The whole collected AGRIS information is distributed using a series of CD-ROMs:

Agrindex is now available in online. India has been participating with it through the Indian Council of Agricultural Research. This is a very valuable information source in agriculture and related subjects. Any library specializing in agro-related subjects should subscribe to this for their clientele.

CHEMICAL ABSTRACTS SERVICES (CAS)

This is a well known abstracting services published from Columbus in Ohio by the American Chemical Society. Chemical Abstracts has been associated with the American Chemical Society in one way or another since 1907. For many years, beginning in 1909, the offices of Chemical Abstracts were housed in various places on the campus of Ohio State University. In 1965, CAS moved to a new 50 acre site just north of the Ohio State campus. In 1907, William A. Noyes was the first editor of the new publication, Chemical Abstracts.

E. J. Crane became the first Director of Chemical Abstracts Service when the organization became an American Chemical Society operational division in 1956. Crane had been its editor since 1915, and his dedication to the organization was a key factor in its long-term success.

Dale B. Baker became the CAS Director upon Crane's retirement in 1958. CAS was an early leader in the use of computer technology to organize and disseminate information.

The CAS Chemical Registry System was introduced in 1965. CAS developed a unique registry number to identify chemical substances. This number registry system would prove to be vital to chemical research, health and safety information, and the communication of chemical information. Robert J. Massie has been the President of CAS since 1992. Many new products and services have been released under his leadership.

Chemical abstracts contain English language abstracts and indexes of world's literature of chemistry and chemical engineering. Approximately 8,000 journals, technical reports, dissertations, conference proceedings and new books in 50 languages, are monitored yearly, as are patent specifications from 27 countries and two international organizations. Chemical Abstracts ceased print publication on January 1, 2010.

Each abstract included in CA provides bibliographical information about the documents like the title, authors with address of the first author, title of periodical, year, volume and issue number, pages, the language of the article and the record number.

The two principal databases that support the different products are CAplus and Registry. CAplus consists of bibliographic information and abstracts for all articles in chemical journals worldwide, and chemistry-related articles from all scientific journals, patents, and other scientific publications.

Registry contains information on more than 50 million organic and inorganic substances, and more than 60 million protein and DNA sequences. The chemical information is produced by CAS; the sequence information comes from CAS and GenBank, (An annotated collection of all publicly available DNA sequence) produced by the National Institutes of Health. The chemical information is prepared by the CAS Registry System, which identifies each compound with a specific CAS registry number, index name, and graphic representation of its chemical structure. The assignment of chemical names is done according to the chemical nomenclature rules for *CA* index names.

The material from these basic and supplementary databases is searchable in many ways. CAS databases are available via two principal database systems, STN, and SciFinder.

STN International (Scientific & Technical Information Network), is a system operated jointly by CAS and Fiz Karlsruhe and is intended primarily for information professionals, using a command language interface rather than a graphics interface. In addition to CAS databases, STN also provides access to many other databases which are similar to other commercial systems such as Dialog.

SciFinder is a CAS database of chemical and bibliographic information. Originally available only as a software client application, a web version was released in 2008. The client version is designed primarily for use by professional chemists in commercial organizations. Versions for both the Windows and Macintosh operating systems are available. SciFinder Scholar is a version designed for universities and other academic institutions and lacks some supplementary features for multi-database searching. Both the commercial and academic versions have a graphics interface, making them particularly suitable for searching the Registry file for chemical structures.

The abstracts are classified according to chemical subjects and are arranged in five broad sections with a total of 80 topical subdivisions.

Chemical abstracts is the major abstracting service in

chemistry and an essential tool in literature searching. It is the most widely used abstracting service in Chemistry and including biochemistry. Because of its extensive coverage, CA will be useful to students and faculty. It will be an invaluable reference in any library. The price of this reference source is however prohibitive.

DEVELOPMENT SCIENCES INFORMATION SYSTEM (DEVSIS)

Development Science Information System (DEVSIS) was started in order to harness the information on social and economic development from all nations for the benefit of the whole humanity. It is a cooperative venture where all the nations of the world work together, each country collecting and processing development information available within its territory. This information relates to various activities related to economic planning, administration, education, health and all other development activities of government agencies and the NGOs in a particular country. The motives for initiating this was:

1. Creation of a new economic and social order for maintaining peace and prosperity in the world. Economic and social balance between various sections of a society and between developed and developing nations has to be corrected and eradication of inequalities of all types to the maximum possible extent.
2. Promoting collaboration between nations for the creation of such a social order.
3. Since knowledge is the catalyst for social change, sharing of knowledge has to be promoted and utilized for reducing social inequities.
4. Advancement in knowledge transfer for promotion of wealth and welfare.

John E Wooston, the director of Information Sciences, of International Development Research Centre (IDRC), Canada, proposed the idea of mooting a cooperative information system in a paper entitled "DEVSIS: A Development Science Information System." In 1974 an international conference was convened in Ottawa in which the proposal for formation of a steering committee and a feasibility study team were made for the purpose of starting DEVSIS. The feasibility study was sponsored by the United Nations Development Programme, Organisation for Economic Cooperation and Development, ILO and UNESCO.

The main objectives of DEVSIS are:

1. To improve access to social and economic information to those engaged in development activities in the developing countries of the world.
2. To achieve coordination between the existing information facilities including libraries
3. To keep abreast with technological advancements in information and communication and utilize this for information services.
4. The formation of an information infrastructure including all published and unpublished materials whereby the input from various sources would be pooled together and decentralized output services will be provided.
5. To trace all published and unpublished documents and data with the help of the participating member countries and promote its perusal by all concerned.
6. To encourage all the nations of the world to give consideration to development information as an integral component of the national information policies.

The feasibility study team was responsible for developing the DEVSIS. This team identified the development information activities and resources in the developed and developing countries of the world in order to define the scope, coverage, inputs and output and the processing of the system. It examined the financial and legal requirements and made proposals for alternative options for implementation.

DEVSIS is a global decentralized mission-oriented information system and not discipline oriented system. Any information that is relevant to the furtherance of social and economic development of the society is included in the system. They include development plans of various governments and non-governmental agencies, statistical and factual information, reports of development projects, policy statements of governments, theoretical studies on socio-economic development, demographic and health aspects of the population etc.

Functioning of DEVSIS

The participating centres collect the information generated within a territory in the country. The records are prepared in a format acceptable to the DEVSIS central unit. The central unit then makes validity checks of the records thus prepared. After validity checks these records are used as the basic unit of the information file for service. Regional participation centres also develop programmes in their regions to support national participants in DEVSIS. The national participating centre identifies and collects nationally produced publications, reports and other documents relevant to the DEVSIS system. It gathers information and records the same in the prescribed form and passes them to the central unit. They record it in their central file and make it available on a global basis. The central unit provides guidelines to the national centres which have to submit copies of the full texts of those items to the central unit.

The records received from the participating centres are converted into computer magnetic tape records using conversion programmes. The master tape is duplicated and sent to subscribers. The central unit has to be located in an organization of the United Nations family. It gives the outputs of DEVSIS like DEVINDEX and its computer tapes. Cumulative versions of DEVSIS files are issued regularly for the benefit of new participants. Subsets of cumulative databases related to geographic sectors, language and subject areas are also generated. Distribution of inverted file of access points to records in databases may also be done by the central unit. The full texts of non-conventional documents input by the national units are also provided on microfiche by the central unit. DEVSIS has two types of files. File 1 contains materials available by citing bibliographic references giving abstracts and key data. This is a comprehensive file. A printed announcement bulletin DEVINDEX and a magnetic tape service are the products of this file. File 2 is a data file on specialized sources and services available that deals with statistical services in particular sectors, ongoing research registers, commodities data available on a global level etc.and is maintained by the Central Unit. Outputs from file 2 called DEVPROFILE, a microfiche back up copy of all the information about the records in file 2, are generated by the central unit. It also undertakes training and advisory services to the national units. The printed product of DEVSIS is a comprehensive bibliography of the records added to the central field in the period between system updates. The references are arranged first by the subject categories and further arranged according to geographic codes.

The UN Department of Economic and Social Affairs is deemed as the most appropriate body to manage DEVSIS. The UNESA has a small information systems unit run in line with

DEVSIS and produces an index to the unpublished reports of this UN department called Development Information Abstracts. The UN Economic Commission for Latin America is endeavoring for a cooperative regional system known as INFOPLAN. In Addis Ababa, the UN Economic Commission for Africa is launching a cooperative regional system called DEVSIS-AFRICA. Botswana is participating in the Pan-African Development Information System and more specifically in the PADIS-DEVSIS program. The principal output from the project will be two issues of Devindex.

The objectives of DEVSIS are laudable in attempting to establish a new economic and social order with special emphasis on the developing countries with the regional and national level participation.

INTERNATIONAL NUCLEAR INFORMATION SYSTEM (INIS)

The **International Nuclear Information System** (INIS) is an information system on the peaceful uses of nuclear science and technology. INIS is operated by the International Atomic Energy Agency (International Atomic Energy Agency) in collaboration with 122 Member States and 24 co-operating international organizations.

It provides a comprehensive information reference service for literature on the peaceful applications of nuclear science and technology. For this INIS processes most of the world's scientific and technical literature that falls within its subject scope and maintains a database which is the world's most comprehensive information source on the peaceful applications of nuclear science and technology.

The history of this data base can be traced back to the US Atomic Energy Commission which existed between 1947-76. During this period there were also a few abstracting journals in nuclear science and related subjects. But due to financial difficulties the activities of all these bodies were in uncertainty. In 1965 two consultants, one from USA and the Soviet Union each were invited by the Director General of IAEA to draw up a plan to establish an agency to monitor the nuclear science literature and monitor nuclear energy activities of all the countries. Its main recommendations included the following points.

1. English would be the medium language of the system.
2. National and regional information services would work in unison for the preparation and dissemination of the products of the system.
3. Input data would be decentralised.
4. It urged the development of an INIS Thesaurus and an indexing instruction manual.

Consequently the IAEA Board of governors agreed to the establishment of an international nuclear information system in Vienna. The participant nations would provide the input data which would be merged into the master file in Vienna and processed for use by individual countries. Thus the information related to nuclear science was globally harnessed and made available to everyone. Thus it conforms to the UNISIST principle of decentralised input and dissemination and centralised processing. It caters to the information needs of the developing countries and gives training to its scientific and technical personnel. Its philosophy is mission-oriented, decentralised operations, specialized document delivery, universality of output products and training and assistance to members. In India the library and information centre at the Bhabha Atomic Research Centre, Mumbai is the national inputting centre for INIS and receives INIS output on Magnetic tapes.

Initially its subject scope was very limited to nuclear science. But later on several penumbral subjects like health, general physics, high energy physics, radiation physics, cosmic radiation, chemistry, earth sciences, radiation side effects environment problems, engineering, cryogenics etc. were also included.

The INIS file contains the reference number, authors and author affiliations, corporate entry, title in English, language of published document, journal title, imprint and collation, International Standard Book Number, conference title, place and date, report number etc. The descriptors are taken from the INIS Thesaurus which was compiled by the European Atomic Energy Community and revised regularly. The data bank contains abstracts of both conventional and non-conventional documents like journal articles, research and development reports, conference papers, books, patents, theses, laws, regulations and standards. INIS inputting centres scan about 4000 journals regularly. The citations and abstracts are in English and over 70 per cent of items referred are in English.

Magnetic tapes containing detailed bibliographic records and subject descriptors are used for its products and services. These are available only for participant member states and organisations.. These magnetic tapes enable selection by subject, title, author, institution, country of origin, date or form of publication etc. and are utilised by member states for producing various information services like retrospective search, SDI services, reference service etc.

Currently, the INIS Database contains over 3 million bibliographic records and almost 200,000 full-text of non-conventional documents, like scientific and technical reports. INIS database also maintains a unique collection of over 300,000 full text non-conventional gray literature that would be difficult to obtain elsewhere.

INIS represents a wealth of experience and an extensive pool of information in the nuclear field. The first INIS output products, the printed Atomindex, a printed semi-monthly bibliography prepared from the magnetic tapes and associated magnetic tapes, were issued in April 1970. Atomindex contains abstracts and is a valuable abstracting journal in the field of nuclear science and related topics. Each issue carries a personal author index, corporate author index, subject index, conference index of standards, reports and patents. INIS has since grown into one of the most successful and comprehensive information systems on the peaceful uses of nuclear science and technology. Since April 2009 INIS has been opened to all Internet users around the world. Free open and unrestricted access is available from the INIS Homepage (http://www.iaea.org/inisnkm). This initiative provides easy access to reliable information on the peaceful uses of nuclear science and technology, including non-conventional literature, and makes nuclear knowledge readily available worldwide.

The IAEA works for the safe, secure and peaceful uses of nuclear science and technology. Its key roles contribute to international peace and security, and to the World's Millennium Goals for social, economic and environmental development. The three main pillars or areas of work on which INIS is founded are:

Safeguards & Verification

The IAEA is the world's nuclear inspectorate, with more than four decades of verification experience. Inspectors work to verify that safeguarded nuclear material and activities are not used for military purposes. The Agency is additionally responsible for the nuclear file in Iraq as mandated by the UN Security Council.

Safety and Security

The IAEA helps countries to upgrade nuclear safety and security, and to prepare for and respond to emergencies. Work is modeled on international conventions, standards and expert guidance. The main aim is to protect people and the environment from harmful radiation exposure.

Science & Technology

The IAEA helps countries to mobilize peaceful applications of nuclear science and technology. The work contributes to goals of sustainable development in fields of energy, environment, health, and agriculture, among others, and to cooperation in key areas of nuclear science and technology. Operated by the IAEA, INIS is based on international cooperation. At present, 122 INIS Member States and 24 international member organizations are members of INIS.

As of May 2009 the INIS Database is freely available world-wide. It offers access to literature on nuclear science and technology published worldwide, covering 1970 to the present, the INIS Database is available online and on CD-ROM. At the end of 2008, the INIS Database included over 3 million references and abstracts of journal articles, scientific and technical reports, conference papers, books, patents, nuclear laws, regulations, theses and web documents. The scope of the INIS Database covers all areas of activities of the IAEA, including nuclear engineering and technology, nuclear safety and radiation protection, safeguards and non-proliferation, applications of nuclear and isotope techniques, nuclear and high energy physics, nuclear and radiation chemistry, nuclear applications in life sciences, legal aspects, and environmental and economic aspects of nuclear and non-nuclear energy sources. The INIS Database also offers access to a unique collection of non-conventional "grey" literature, with over 850 000 full-text documents in 63 languages. It includes many documents that are not available in the public domain. The NCL collection is accessible via the INIS Online Database and also available on CD-ROM.

INIS has published several documents so far in INIS Reference Series. This series defines the rules, standards, formats, codes and authority lists approved by INIS. These are useful and essential tools for cataloguers, indexers, abstractors and researchers. These are prescriptions necessary for maintaining standardization and compatibility with other systems and for preparation of input. Manuals necessary for nuclear science related **activities are revised from time to time for the benefit of global users.**

MEDICAL LITERATURE ANALYSIS AND RETRIEVAL SYSTEM (MEDLARS)

MEDLARS (Medical Literature Analysis and Retrieval System) is a computerised biomedical bibliographic retrieval system. It is a relational database of the United States National Library of Medicine for the storage and retrieval of Medical Literature. It was initiated by John Shaw Billings, head of the Library of the Surgeon General's Office. This library later evolved into the United Publication in 1879 and continued monthly through 1926, with a hiatus between 1899 and 1902. During this hiatus, a similar index, the Bibliographia Medica, was published in French by the Institut de Bibliographie in Paris. The Index Medicus was amalgamated with the American Medical Association's Quarterly Cumulative Index as the Quarterly Cumulative Index Medicus in 1927. The American Medical Association continued to publish this until 1956. In May 1962, accompanied by armed Pinkerton guards, the collection was moved from Cleveland to the Library's current location in Bethesda, Maryland.

From 1960 to 2004 the printed edition was published by the National Library of Medicine under the name Index Medicus/Cumulated Index Medicus (IM/CIM). An abridged version was published from 1970 to 1997 as the Abridged

Index Medicus. The abridged edition lives on as a subset of the journals covered by "'Pubmed 'or "core clinical journals." The last issue of Index Medicus was published in December 2004 (Volume 45). The stated reason for discontinuing the printed publication was that online resources had supplanted it, most especially PubMed, which continues to include the Index as a subset of the journals it covers.

Selection of journals into the Index is not automatic and depends on a journal's scientific policy and scientific quality. These criteria are evaluated by the "Literature Selection Technical Review Committee" and the final decision is made by the NLM director. The review process may include outside reviewers and journals may also be dropped from inclusion. Each article included in the Index Medicus is given as many subject headings as required. The subject Headings are selected from a controlled vocabulary called Medical Subject Headings (MeSH) which is published and revised annually as part two of the January issue of the Index Medicus. The latest information on biomedical subjects is selected to keep abreast with the mainstream of development.

The National Library of Medicine provided computer based system for biomedical reference storage and retrieval with the development of Medical Literature Analysis and Retrieval System (MEDLARS) since January 1964. This helped to improve the quality of Index Medicus and to allow fast searching of the large computer store of references.

The online bibliographic retrieval system known as MEDLINE (MEDLARS Online) was initiated in October 1971. Medline is a pioneering online bibliographic database containing more than 70,00000 citation from 3500 recent medical periodicals from 70 countries. During 2005-2009 alone a total of 3,219,081 citations were added to Medline.

About 30,000 citations are added to the basic database every month. Medline incorporates all of Index Medicus, Index to Dental Literature and International Nursing Index covering research practice, administration, policy issues, health care service, dental research and nursing information.

Now MEDLINE is also available on CD-ROM which is a big boon to Index Medicus users world-wide. The National Medical Library of India provides this indexing service on CD-ROM in India. The National Informatics Centre is designated as the Indian Medlars nationwide satellite computer communication network providing the Medlars service.

Index Medicus is considered as an excellent and indispensable indexing service for students and faculty in and allied subjects. It has become renowned and accessible to the entire world by its online and CD-ROM services.

It was launched by the National Library of Medicine in 1964 and was the first large scale, computer based, retrospective search service available to the general public. In 1971 an online version called MEDLINE ("MEDLARS Online") became available.

Since 1879, the National Library of Medicine (NLM) has published Index Medicus, a monthly guide to medical articles in thousands of journals. The huge volume of bibliographic citations were manually compiled. In 1957 the staff of the NLM started to plan the mechanization of the Index Medicus; what was needed was a way to manipulate all this information to produce subsidiary products. By 1960 a detailed specification was prepared and by 1961 a request for proposals was sent out to 72 companies to develop the system. As a result a contract was awarded to the General Electric Company. The computer (Minneapolics Honeywell 800) which was to run MEDLARS was delivered to the NLM in March 1963. MEDLARS cost $3 million to develop and at the time of its completion no other publicly available, fully operational electronic storage and retrieval system of its magnitude existed. The original computer configuration operated from 1964 until its replacement by MEDLARS II in January 1975.

UNISIST

In 1948 UNESCO sponsored a conference on indexing and abstracting in biological and medical sciences and another conference in 1949 on scientific abstracting. The deliberations of these conferences paved way to the founding of the International Council of Scientific Unions (ICSU). In 1959 another conference there was on scientific information. Two of its participants, W.Chamberlin and P Boquet mooted the idea of a world institute for scientific information. Mr. Chamberlin suggested that this institute has to provide all scientists at all levels with all the information that they need.. The storage and retrieval of scientific information cannot be controlled by governments and has to be controlled by scientists themselves but the government has to provide financial assistance to the same. The policies of the institute could be set by a body such as the General Conference of UNESCO but the executive policy should be determined by scientists themselves.

The aims of such an institute as suggested by Boquet were:

1. To ensure cooperation of all documentation centres controlled by the state and other organizations.
2. Employing advanced methods to collect, classify, select, preserve, translate and reproduce scientific information.
3. To organize symposia and conferences and publish their reports.

4. To publish indexes, tables of contents and summaries of papers in periodicals.
5. To carry out bibliographical work for scientific institutions, laboratories and offices of various industries.
6. To unify and improve documentation methods
7. To foster relations between all scientists by publishing directory of research centres and specialists.

Subsequently the ICSU and UNESCO held two separate conferences and the two bodies agreed to study the feasibility of World Scientific Information System. This was approved by the General Conference of UNESCO. The intergovernmental conference for the establishment of a world science Information system took place at UNESCO head quarters in Paris in 1971. The conference focused on the various aspects of establishment of the UNISIST. The basic philosophy behind UNISIST is the same as that of UNESCO such as diffusion of knowledge, encouraging cooperation among the nations in all branches of intellectual activity, exchange of publications, to give the people of all countries access to the printed and published materials. UNISIST is an international effort for free flow of scientific and technical. information. In November 1972 the UNESCO General Conference authorized the establishment of UNISIST programme with the following goals.

1. To advance and coordinate the world trends towards information sharing and cooperative agreements among governments, international organizations and operating information services.
2. To provide guidance and initiate action for the necessary development in the field of scientific and technical information.

3. To facilitate the access of published information to scientists, engineers and technologists.
4. To help the developing countries meet their needs for scientific and technical information.

UNISIST has undertaken many programmes and projects since its inception. One of its important programmes was the "Information Dissemination: Methods and Standards." This programmme is aiming at preparation and distribution of guidelines and manuals of practice, the creation and maintenance of specialized centres and systems and institution based activities. It also supports creation of technical standards. Reference Manual for Machine Readable Bibliographic Description, International Standards Bibliographic Description for General Monographs, Universal MARC Format(UNIMARC), Guidelines for Editors of Scientific Journals are some of the important publications made by the UNISIST. It has also made very commendable work in the area of networking by creating the International Serials Data System (ISDS), the International Information Centre for Terminology (INFOTERM)(Austria), the International Centre for Bibliographic Description, (England) etc. ISDS is used for identification of all serial publication by providing an International Standard Serial Number. INFOTERM collects and disseminates highly specialized information on terminological standards, publication, projects and courses. These activities have contributed significantly towards developments in information transfer.

UNISIST has rendered invaluable help to the developing countries in adopting the national requirements for scientific and technical information, imparting training and educating the manpower, advising on national information policy, modernizing the scientific and technical documentation and information centres etc. In 1976 UNISIST supported a demonstration of online access to remote data bases at Tata

Institute of Fundamental Research with the help of European Space Agency Information Centre. It has assisted the developing countries in getting financial assistance from the UNDP for projects related to the dissemination of scientific and technical information.

UNISIST has helped the libraries and documentation centres in the world by sharing of workloads and elimination of duplication. Scientific and technical workers and students were able to get exposure to the latest developments in their field.

The National Information Systems (NATIS) were integrated with UNISIST. Therefore the duplication of work in individual countries were avoided. The UNESCO General Conference held in Nairobi in 1976 approved the merger of NATIS and UNISIST. This merger resulted in the birth of the General Information Programme (PGI/UNISIST-II) which replaced the activities of UNISIST-I and NATIS.

The PGI/UNISIST-II had three organs. i) The Intergovernmental Council which is responsible for guiding programme planning and monitoring. The council consists of 30 member states of UNESCO and meets once in two years for deliberations on the programmes and its implementation and approve the budget. ii) The Executive Office which is responsible to the Assistant Director General for Studies and Programming. iii) The Advisory Committee.

PGI has published some important works that help information processing and dissemination like ISO Standards Handbook- Information Transfer (Ed 2, 1982), A reference Manual for Machine Readable Bibliographic Descriptions (Ed 3, 1981), A Reference Manual for Machine Readable Descriptions of Research Projects and Institutions, 1982, and Common Communication Format (ed 3,1993). It was PGI that developed the mini version of Computerised Documentation System/Integrated Set of Information Systems (CDS/ISIS) and the software package made available to the libraries in the developing countries. It has also given assistance to about fifty projects about software, consultation, equipment and training for creation of databases. It has helped the establishment of Regional Network for the Exchange of Information and Experience in Science and Technology in Asia-Pacific (ASTINFO) and Asia-Pacific Information Network in Social Sciences (APINESS). The PGI training programmes have helped the improvement of skills of the library and information personnel.

BIOSCIENCES INFORMATION SYSTEM (BIOSIS)

BIOSIS research database provides with today's most current sources of life sciences information, including journals, conferences, patents, books, review articles, and the like. You can access multidisciplinary coverage via specialized indexing such as MeSH disease terms, CAS Registry Numbers, Sequence Databank Numbers and Major Concepts. It is an independent non-profit organisation which works in unison with many biological institutions and societies like the National Academy of Sciences, the American Association for the Advancement of Science, the American Institute of Biological Sciences and the Federation of American Societies for Experimental Biology. It was originally founded in 1926, and the name was changed to BioSciences Information Service of Biological Abstracts (BIOSIS) in 1964.

BIOSIS is the world's largest life science abstracting, indexing and access service and disseminates information in suitable formats to cater to the needs of life science researchers. The literature covers original biological research reports and reviews of literature. Articles from inter-disciplinary journals are also included. It publishes Biological Abstracts and The Zoological Record and has published over a hundred other science publications. In 2004 the company was purchased by Thomson Scientific and it is now part of Thomson Reuters Science & Healthcare division. Thomson relabeled BIOSIS with the interim name "The J.R.S. Foundation", but it is still referred to generally as BIOSIS.

The Information Products and Services of BIOSIS

Biological Abstracts includes the whole spectrum of life sciences and is classified into 650 topics and issued as a bi-monthly. There are four computer generated indexes in these issues. They are BASIC (a subject index - keyword in context), generated by permutation of the title and supplementary keywords; Cross index based on specific subject concept; Biosystematic Index containing the taxonomic categories; the author index.

In 2007, Wolters Kluwer announced the digital availability of the BIOSIS Archive and Zoological Record Archive databases, via their Ovid Technologies online services. The BIOSIS Archive consists of the data from the print volumes of Biological Abstracts from 1926 to 1968, and the Zoological Record Archive contains the data published in print in the Zoological Record from 1864 to 1977. In 2010 Biosis Citation Index was released on the Web of Knowledge Platform, combining extensive indexing and database coverage of Biosis Previews with the Web of Science's citation tracking features. The following information products are in vogue among the research community:

i) Bioresearch Index

ii) List of Serials

iii) Bioresearch Today

iv) Biological Abstracts on Microfilm

v) Biological Abstracts Previews

vi) Abstracts of Mycology

vii) Current Literature Alerting Search Service

viii) Retrospective Search Service

REFERENCES

Atherton,P: Handbook of information systems and services. Paris, UNESCO, 1977.

Bhatt, R.K. : Information Systems. New Delhi, Pragati, 2009.

Kumar, PSG: Fundamentals of Information Science. New Delhi, S.Chand.Co, 1998

Neelameghan, A: DEVSIS: A global information system for socio-economic development. Lib. Sci. 12,1975. pp55-64.

Bibliography

Atherton,P: Handbook of Information systems and services. Paris, UNESCO, 1977

Bhatt, R.K: Information systems. New Delhi, Pragati Publications,2009.

Bhattacharyya,G: Information Science : A unified view through a system approach. Calcutta, IASLIC, 1978.

Bonn, George S : Literature of Science and technology. In McGraw Hill

Borchers, Jan O. Electronic Books: definition, genres, and interaction design patterns. (http://readingonline.org).

Borko, H: Information Science: What is it? American Documentation. January, 1968.

Bose,H: Information Science: Principles and practice. New Delhi, Sterling, 1986.

Bourne, R: IFLA International programme for UBC. IFLA

journal.12, 1986.pp.341-43.

Britain, JM: Information and its users. Bath, Bath University, 1970.

Crawford, Susan: Information needs of user. ARIST.13,1978.

Cronin, Blaise: Assessing user needs. Aslib Proceedings. 33(2) 1981. P.37-47.

Davis, RA and Bailey: Bibliography of user studies. Philadelphia, Drexel Institute of Technology, 1964

Devarajan,G,Ed: Bibliometric studies. New Delhi, ESS ESS, 1997.

Dhiman, Anil K and Yashoda Rani: Learn information and reference sources and services.New Delhi, ESS ESS, 2005.

Documentation Research and Training Centre(Bangalore): Seminar on Reference Service: Working papers and Proceedings, Bangalore, DRTC, 1971. Encyclopaedia of Science and Technology. V7.New York, McGraw -Hill, 1971.

Encyclopedia Britanica.ed.15.v.6-Micropedia.Chicago, Encyclopedia Britanica Inc. 1993.

Fjallbrant, N and Stevenson, M: User education in libraries. London, Clive Bingly.1978.

Fjallbrant, Nancy and Stevenson,Malcolm: User education in libraries.London, Clive Bingly, 1978.

Fleming, Hugh, Ed: User education in academic libraries.London,LA, 1990

Foskett, DJ: Information service in libraries. Ed.2.Connecticut, Archon Books, 1967.

Gates, JK: Guide to the use of libraries and information sources.New York, McGraw-Hill, 1979.

Gelfand, MA : University libraries for developing countries. Paris, UNESCO, 1968.

Grogan, Denis: Science and technology: An introduction to the literature. London,Bingly, 1982.

Guha, B: Documentation and Information. Calcutta, World Press, 1978.

Guichat, G and Monou, M: General introduction to the techniques of information and documentation work. Paris, UNESCO, 1983.

Gupta, BM and Jain,VK,Ed: Handbook of Libraries, Archives and Information cenres in India.Vol.8, Delhi, Aditya Prakashan,1985.

Guskin, Allen E, et al: The academic library as a teaching library : a role for the 1980s. Library Trends, 1979.

Hamilton, D and Parlett, M: Evaluatin as illumination. In D Tawney,ed. Curriculum evaluation today: trends and implications. London, Macmillan, 1976.

Harrod's Librarians' Glossary and Reference Book.ed.5.USA, Gower pub.Co.1984..

Harrod's Librarians' Glossary of terms used in librarianship documentation, and the book crafts and reference Book. Ed.5.USA, Gower Pub.Co.1984.

Harrod's Librarians' Glossary.ed8.England, Gower, 1995.

Hills, R J, Ed: Information package on teaching methods for librarians. London, The British Library, 1979.

Katz, WA: Introduction to reference work. New York, McGraw-Hill, 1982.

Kirk, Thomas G: Bibliographic instruction - a review of research'. In conference on the Evaluation of library instruction, Denver(1973). Evaluating library instruction. ed.by Richar B Beeler, Michigan, Pierian Press, 1975.

Krishan Kumar. Reference service. New Delhi, Vikas,2008.

Kumar, PSG: Information sources and services: Theory and practice. New Delhi, BR Publishing Corporation, 2004.

Kumar, PSG: Fundamentals of Information Science. New Delhi, S.Chand.Co,

Kunz, Werner, et al : Methods of analysis and evaluation of information needs. Munchen, Verlag Documentation, 1977.

Lewis, David and Foster, Allan: Tuition in library and literature use.In George Jefferson and GCK Smith-Bunett. The college library. London,Clive Bingly, 1978

Lipetz, Ben-Ami: Information needs and users. ARIST.5, 1970.

Lubans, John: Educating the library use. New York, R R Bowker,1974.

Luhn, HP: selective dissemination of new scientific information with the aid of electronic processing equipment. American Documentation.12(1) 1961.

Machlup,F and Mansfield,U: Study of information, interdisciplinary messages. New York, Wiley.1983.

McGarry,KJ: Changing context of information: An introductory analysis.London, Clive Bingly.1981.p.13.

Mckee, Bob: Information studies. Libr. Ass. Rec. 1986. 88(5) pp. 236-39.

Miller, Stuart Wayne: Library use instruction in selected American colleges.Illinois, University of Illinois Graduaate school of Library Science,1978.

Molhot,Pat: The nature of information and its influence on

libraries. Special Libraries. July 1984.p.247.

Neelameghan, A: DEVSIS: A global information systemfor socio-economic development.Lib.Sci.12,1975.pp55-64.

Paisely, JM: Information needs and uses. ARIST.3, 1968.

Prasher,RG: Information and communication. ILA Bulletin 23(3)1987.p.18.

Prytherch, Ray,Comp: Harrod' Librarians' Glossary.. England, Gower, 1995.

Ranaganathan, SR: Reference Service. Bombay, Asia publishing, 1961.

Random House Dictionary of English Language. New York, Random House,1966

Ranganathan,SR: Reference service and bibliography. Madras, Madras Library Association, 1940

Sehal, RL: User education in computer based libraries.New Delhi, ESS ESS1998.

Shaw, Ralph: Pilot study on the use of scientific literature by scientists. Washington, National Science Foundation, 1965.

Shores, William: Basic reference sources. Chicago, ALA, 1954

Stevenson, M B: User education programmes. Boston.Spa. The British Library, 1977.

Weisman, HM: Information systems, services and centres. New York, Becker, 1972.

Whittaker, Kenneth: The basis of library based user services. London, LA, 1993.

Wilson, TD: Guidelines for developing and implementing a

national plan for training and information. Paris, UNESCO, 1968.

Winchel, CM: Guide to reference books. Chicago, ALA

Wysoki, A : Study of users' information needs: subject and methods of FID on theoretical problems of informatics. Moscow, All Union Institute for Scientific and Technical Information, 1969.

Index

instruction. ed. by Richard B Beeler, Michigan: Pierian Press, 1975.

Kushal Kumar. Reference Service. New Delhi: Vikas, 2004.

Kumar, PSG. Information sources and services: theory and practice. New Delhi: BR Publishing Corporation, 2004.

Kumar, PSG. Fundamentals of Information Science. New Delhi: S.Chand, [illegible]

Kunz, Werner, et al. Methods of analysis and evaluation of information needs. München: Verlag Dokumentation, 1977.

Lewis, David and Foster, Allan. Tuition in library and literature use in Colleges. Jefferson, and D.C. Smith. [illegible] The college library. London: Clive Bingley, 1978.

Lipetz, Ben Ami. Information needs and users. ARIST [illegible] 1970.

Lubans, John. Educating the library user. New York: R.R. Bowker, 1974.

Luhn, HP. Selective dissemination of new scientific information with the aid of electronic processing equipment. American Documentation 12(1) 1961.

Machlup, F. and Mansfield, U. Study of information: interdisciplinary messages. New York: Wiley, 1983.

Mcgarry, K. Changing context of information: An introductory analysis. London: Clive Bingley, 1981.

McKee, Bob. Information studies. Lib. Ass. Rec. 1986, 88(5) pp. [illegible]

Miller, Stuart Wayne. Library use instruction in selected American colleges. Illinois: University of Illinois Graduate School of Library Science, 1978.

Mohd. Riaz. Generation of information and its [illegible]